Prais
Overcoming Dysthymia and Chronic Mild Depression

"Easy to read about, tough to put into practice, Thase's strategies for feeling better are worth the time and effort."

—*Chicago Tribune*

"If you need help lifting the veil of gloom and apathy, this is the best concise guide to treating chronic depression I have seen."

—James H. Kocsis, M.D.,
Professor of Psychiatry, Cornell Medical Center

"Stop weeping into your Cheerios and do something to help yourself. If you've been chalking up your fatigue, irritation, pessimism, and anti-social behavior to a mood swing, surprise—that mood swing you've had for fifteen years may actually be dysthymia. More subtle than severe depression, Dysthymia is a mild version of the disorder that lasts for more than two years. The easy-to-read '*Blues*' describes therapies, medications, and alternative approaches that can help you feel better."

—*New York Daily News*

"Michael Thase is unique in that he has internationally renowned expertise both in medication treatment and in psychotherapy for depression. He writes clearly and colorfully. This book on chronic depression, a troubling affliction that is too often ignored, is a masterpiece. I couldn't put it down."

—Robert M.A. Hirschfeld, M.D.,
Titus H. Harris Chair, Professor and Chair,
Department of Psychiatry and Behavioral Sciences,
University of Texas Medical Branch at Galveston

"This book is a step forward. Dr. Thase is an expert in depression, with a wealth of clinical experience, scholarly knowledge, and a scientist's incisive judgment. His research encompasses both biological and psychotherapeutic treatments. The reader of *Beating the Blues* can trust what he or she learns. This book helps bridge the gap between knowledge and its practical application to heal."

—Alan J. Gelenberg, M.D.,
Professor and Head, Department of Psychiatry,
University of Arizona College of Medicine, and
Founding Editor of *Biological Therapies in Psychiatry Newsletter*, and
Editor-in-Chief, *The Journal of Clinical Psychiatry*

BEATING THE BLUES

New Approaches to Overcoming Dysthymia and Chronic Mild Depression

Michael E. Thase, M.D.
and
Susan S. Lang

OXFORD
UNIVERSITY PRESS

OXFORD
UNIVERSITY PRESS

Oxford University Press, Inc., publishes works that
further Oxford University's objective of excellence
in research, scholarship, and education.

Oxford   New York
Auckland Cape Town Dar es Salaam   Hong Kong   Karachi
Kuala Lumpur Madrid Melbourne Mexico City Nairobi
New Delhi Shanghai Taipei Toronto

With offices in
Argentina Austria Brazil Chile Czech Republic France Greece
Guatemala Hungary Italy Japan Poland Portugal Singapore
South Korea Switzerland Thailand Turkey Ukraine Vietnam

Copyright © 2004 by Oxford University Press, Inc.

First published by Oxford University Press, Inc., 2004
198 Madison Avenue, New York, NY 10016
www.oup.com

First issued as an Oxford University Press paperback, 2006
ISBN-13: 978-0-19-530453-4
ISBN-10: 0-19-530453-5

Oxford is a registered trademark of Oxford University Press

The library of Congress has catalogued the cloth edition as follows:
Thase, Michael E.
Beating the blues : new approaches to overcoming dysthymia
and chronic mild depression /
by Michael E. Thase and Susan S. Lang.
p. ; cm.
ISBN-13: 978-0-19-515918-7   ISBN-10: 0-19-515918-7
1. Depression, Mental—Popular works. 2. Affective disorders—
Popular works. 3. Mood (Psychology)
[DNLM: 1. Dysthymic Disorder—rehabilitation—Popular Works.
2. Depressive Disorder—rehabilitation—Popular Works.
WM 171 T367b 2003]
I. Title: New approaches to overcoming dysthymia
and chronic mild depression.
II. Lang, Susan S. III. Title.
RC537 .T477 2003
616.85'27—dc21
2003006657

Excerpt from "Back" ©1966 by the Estate of Jane Kenyon.
Reprinted from *Otherwise: New Selected Poems* with the
permission of Graywolf Press, Saint Paul, Minnesota.

1 3 5 7 9 8 6 4 2
Printed in the United States of America

For my parents, Carl and Evelyn Thase,
for giving me a good start in life
M.E.T.

For Tom and Julia, who buoy my spirits by being there,
and for Bea (in memoriam)
S.S.L.

Contents

Preface

This book is a collaboration of a leading depression researcher and an award-winning, longtime science writer. Our purpose is to raise awareness that suffering from chronic, low-grade depression does not have to be a way of life. Low-grade depression corrodes the quality of life of millions of people, with most never realizing that they have a highly treatable condition.

It is not normal to be apathetic, passive, glum, sad, irritable, joyless, hopeless, helpless, or negative, even for relatively brief periods of time. In this book we focus on chronic forms of depression, which can last years or decades. People who chronically have these feelings suffer from a condition as legitimate as anemia, gastric reflux, or arthritis—if you do nothing about it you may periodically feel okay, but the problem probably won't go away by itself, and in the long term, it could become debilitating.

We have written this book to be as readable as possible, since we know that depression can affect even the best reader's attention span. Our purpose is to inform and motivate readers to take action, not to serve as a reference book for scholars. Therefore, we do not footnote each statistic (which usually vary from study to study, depending on methodology) but, rather, refer the reader seeking sources to an extensive bibliography, the appendices, or the ever-changing body of literature on depression available on the Internet or via the free medical database sponsored by the government: http://www.ncbi.nlm.nih.gov/PubMed/.

Chronic, low-grade depression—dysthymia—is defined as a disorder when a person suffers from more than three symptoms for two years or longer. Yet quality of life is still impaired—needlessly—in millions of people who suffer from milder or shorter forms of depression. The strategies described in this book can be helpful to anyone who wants to lead a lighter, brighter life.

Michael E. Thase, M.D.
Susan S. Lang

Acknowledgments

MET: I want to acknowledge the superhuman efforts and dedication of SSL, who had the vision for this book and the forlorn task of trying to keep me on time (that is, at least to within months of the original deadlines). I also wish to thank my best teachers along the way (Chuck Murdoch, Martin Moss, Ian Gregory, and Jon Himmelhoch) and my longtime mentor and boss (David Kupfer), who has given me the academic freedom to do interesting things. Christine Johnson and Lisa Stupar must be acknowledged for their Herculean efforts to manage my office (and career). Last, I want to thank my patients and their families for helping me learn what I know (and be humble about what I don't know) and extending the privilege and opportunity to keep on learning.

SSL: I wish to thank our Oxford editor, Joan Bossert, whose vision identified a need for this important book, and Tom Schneider, a wonderful cognitive psychotherapist who also is my husband. His input helped shape many of our draft chapters, and his support provided the space I needed to write the book. I also want to thank my dear friends Liz Bauman and Nancy Rosen for their insightful comments, and my daughter, Julia Schneider, and my parents, Beatrice and Solon J. Lang, for too many reasons to list here.

BEATING THE BLUES

PART ONE

◆ ◆ ◆

Understanding Dysthymia and Its Milder Forms

1

♦ ♦ ♦

What Is Dysthymia?

> How heavy the days are,
> There is not a fire
> That can warm me,
> Not a sun to laugh with me.
>
> —Hermann Hesse, *Steppenwolf*

When was the last time you felt vibrant and energized by a job well done, shared laughter and warmth with a loved one, hummed in the shower, and, although it may sound corny, felt that there was a skip in your step? Do you still feel that your life is purposeful, that you feel pretty much in control, and that you actively love—and feel loved by—your friends and family with trusting, positive relationships?

That's how you can—and should—feel.

This book focuses on how to take charge of your moods and the thoughts that create depressive moods as soon as you recognize that

- You have become sluggish mentally or physically
- You are spending more days feeling down than up
- You get less and less pleasure from the things that used to bring you joy
- You feel critical, dull, negative, resentful, or passive

Living in the Gray Zone

We all know how we want to feel—loving, well loved, and upbeat as we work toward our goals in life. We also want to feel content with ourselves. But life is hard. Parents neglect us or die young; peers, teachers, and bosses humiliate us; we get our hearts broken; we fail exams, get fired, fall ill; our children get sick, sometimes they die. Planes crash, terrorists lurk, wars rage, innocent people get murdered, and perpetrators go unpunished—the list of stressful events and traumatic horrors, such as 9/11, is horrific and can challenge our sense of well-being.

You may be the kind of person who stays cheerful, tries again, and gets on with life, enjoying its rich pleasures and interesting people along the way, despite rejection, failures, and losses. If you are reading this book, though, you are likely the type of person who broods about what went wrong, makes mountains out of molehills, blames yourself, feels worthless and helpless, and is feeling numb to the simple joys in daily life.

Without realizing it, you spend more time feeling down than up and soon feel too tired, sluggish, or apathetic to do anything about it or to do other things that would make you feel better. You fret about recent failures or humiliations, scold yourself repeatedly about what you should have done or said, or get down on yourself for not having the energy or drive to do what you know you should be doing. You go out less often, don't finish projects, and stop extending yourself; you don't treat your loved ones or yourself to special kindnesses. Soon, guilt and passivity set in, and because you're less productive, you feel less worthy and lousier and lousier.

This is the downward spiral of negative, pessimistic thinking that can saturate your life. This mild depression can persist for years, flattening your moods and making you much more prone to major depression.

Mental health experts now understand that one key to the two views of life—optimistic or pessimistic—is your style of self-talk, that is, how you talk to yourself in your mind, which can either inoculate you against persistent blues or knock you down toward depression. Is your glass always half full or half empty?

How Mild Depressions Become Chronic

Although many people would recognize a major change in mood, well-being, and sleep or eating patterns (symptoms of major depression), mild depression creeps in so insidiously that you often don't notice anything is wrong. You come to accept life through a gray-tinted lens, but since you get by, you think, "That's just the way I am. That's the way life is. There's really not much I can do about it." You still take part in life

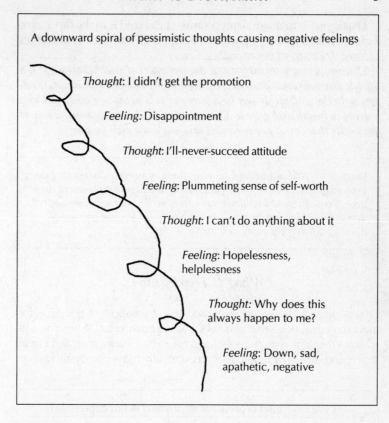

A downward spiral of pessimistic thoughts causing negative feelings

Thought: I didn't get the promotion

Feeling: Disappointment

Thought: I'll-never-succeed attitude

Feeling: Plummeting sense of self-worth

Thought: I can't do anything about it

Feeling: Hopelessness, helplessness

Thought: Why does this always happen to me?

Feeling: Down, sad, apathetic, negative

and even smile along the way, but what you might not have noticed is that you're not reaping much pleasure any more from things that used to bring you joy. You have become tired, irritable, and negative.

You may think this is normal for you and that nothing can change your "nature," but the good news is you are *totally wrong*. When mild depression persists, it is called *dysthymia*. No one knows how many millions suffer on and off from major and minor bouts of depression; some estimates are as high as one-quarter of the population. As for dysthymia, although millions suffer from it, most don't know it. It is one of the most underrecognized and undertreated mood disorders (mental health experts didn't even give it a name until 1980), yet it *is* treatable. In many cases, people can help themselves to some extent. In most cases, psychotherapy or medication or both together can reliably lift the veil of darkness.

Dysthymia is to major depression as a head cold is to the flu or even a life-threatening case of pneumonia. But it's a bad head cold and it's chronic. It seems to never really go away.

Dysthymia saps your energy and changes many of your behaviors. It is a lifestyle destroyer that causes distress, deforms self-image, and disrupts inter-personal relationships. It can be a gateway to a myriad of other problems bearing ill health and despair. You can either do something about it now or anticipate that it will get worse and take you down even further.

Janet, a 47-year-old college administrator, remembers becoming depressed about ten years earlier, after her divorce and a subsequent abortion. "I couldn't find anything I was interested in. I wanted to get excited about something but just couldn't. I had given up somewhere along the way but don't remember when or where."

What Is Dysthymia?

Dysthymia is a chronically depressed mood for most of the day—for more days than not—that persists for at least two years. When you suffer from the same symptoms for longer than two weeks, it's called a mild depression, which, if ignored, often eventually turns into dysthymia.

Do you have mild depression? dysthymia? major depression?

☐ Do you feel sad, blue, or down in the dumps more often than not?

☐ Have these blues been going on for more than two years (one year for children or teens) with no more than a couple of months of relief at a time?

If so, do you also:
  ☐ eat too much or too little?
  ☐ suffer sleeplessness or sleep too much?
  ☐ lack energy, feel tired all the time?
  ☐ have feelings of inadequacy, guilt, or put yourself down all the time?
  ☐ seem less effective or productive at home, school, or work?
  ☐ have trouble concentrating or making decisions?
  ☐ not want to be social much anymore?

(continues)

☐ rarely enjoy or feel interested in pleasurable activities?
☐ get irritated easily?
☐ tend to brood about things, feel sorry for yourself or feel pessimistic about the future?
☐ feel prone to crying?
☐ think about your own death or suicide?*

If the answer is yes to

    2 or 3 of these questions (and for at least 2 weeks), you may have *mild depression*

    2 or more questions for at least two years, you may have *dysthymia*

    5 or more questions for at least two weeks, you may have *major depression*

*If you answered yes to the question about suicidal thoughts, seek help immediately!

If you scored high enough for major depression or if you've been depressed long enough to qualify for dysthymia, *consult your family physician or a mental health professional immediately.* You don't have to suffer. It's important to consult a professional not only for treatment but also to find out whether your symptoms are caused by a medical illness or a medication you may be using.

A major reason why dysthymia goes unrecognized is because you can be depressed without feeling unusually sad or emotionally hurt. Someone who doesn't sleep well, can't enjoy things, can't concentrate, is irritable and always tired may be dysthymic.

THE RISKS OF DOING NOTHING

If you do nothing about living with even a few depressive symptoms, you are at an ever-increasing risk of developing dysthymia.

If you do nothing about dysthymia:

- Your chances of just feeling better out of the blue without trying to help yourself is only about 10 percent.
- Your chances of being depressed 10 years from now is 50 percent. The average time that people live with dysthymia before getting help is more than 20 years.
- Your risk of a major depression within 1 year is 10 percent—75 percent in 5 years. Major depression can be very serious; if left untreated, major depression can be life threatening—more than half of those with untreated depression attempt suicide.

If you don't develop major depression and just remain dysthymic, your risks of feeling worse with more symptoms, of poorer functioning, and even of attempting suicide (the incidence of suicide among people with dysthymia is estimated between 3 to 12 percent) keep increasing. Your risk of being hospitalized in 5 years for psychological reasons is even higher than for someone who experiences periodic major depressions. That may be because with dysthymia your risk of developing other psychiatric conditions in the future is 75 percent.

Untreated dysthymia increases your risks for heart disease, stroke, breast cancer, substance abuse, compromised immune function, and even earlier death. It's also linked to a lifetime of chronic illness, recurring major depression, and substance abuse. Your risks also spike for interpersonal problems, eating disorders, anxiety disorders, divorce, lost productivity, and job failure. For example, 8 out of 10 people with dysthymia report that their problems are so overwhelming that they have serious social problems and/or have trouble doing their jobs well. Your chances for having a longstanding, happy marriage are less than 30 percent.

Children and teens with untreated dysthymia are also at great risk; they have more than a 60 percent chance of experiencing a major depression within 5 years. Their risk of abusing alcohol, drugs, or cigarettes also jumps.

Why does dysthymia impact health so profoundly? Probably because it causes stress and triggers biochemical processes that either deplete or flood the brain with certain chemicals (neurotransmitters and hormones) that are linked to depression. People who are depressed also tend to exercise less and don't eat as well as those who aren't depressed.

"I was plagued by this feeling of pointlessness," says John, 48. "I had no reason to be sad. But I had this overwhelming sense that my life was meaningless."

YOU ARE NOT ALONE

Dysthymia and other forms of depression are not caused by character flaws. They are mood disorders, and rates of mood disorders have increased significantly over the past five decades, becoming the most common mental health problem in the country. Although it is not clear how much of this increase is the result of greater awareness and better recognition of depressive disorders, it has been shown that even mild depression and dysthymia as they are now defined (see chapter 3) are associated with at least as much disability and day-to-day impairment in quality of life as many common illnesses.

Up to one-quarter of Americans at any time experience some depressive symptoms or a mild depression, which means that many are well on the path to dysthymia and depression. If you continue to live with dysthymia, you have a 75 percent chance of joining the 20 percent of Americans (almost 15 percent of men and about one-quarter of all women) who will develop depression within 5 years.

Even though you're living in quiet desperation, chances are you haven't taken it seriously enough. Because dysthymia is low-grade and persistent, you might believe that it's your nature. Also, people sometimes blame their symptoms (such as irritability, sluggishness, or fatigue) on not getting enough sleep or exercise or on a lousy diet. Meanwhile, dysthymia is slowly corroding your quality of life into a bleak grind of colorless days. You get so worn down, you don't even bother thinking about how life used to be or you're too ashamed, or resistant, to ask for help.

Three times more common in women than in men, dysthymia not only makes you miserable and wastes years of your life but makes you much more likely to develop all kinds of problems, from divorce and problematic relationships to job failure, depression, drug and alcohol abuse, and various diseases.

In fact, dysthymia—with its unrelenting and somewhat disabling symptoms—causes more impairment in day-to-day life than diabetes, lung disorders, peptic ulcer, high blood pressure, back problems, and arthritis. Dysthymia also doubles the risk of fatal heart disease.

Having dysthymia is like having a chronic bacterial infection—you can still function but you feel lousy, and there's a significant risk that if you don't do anything about it, it will get worse, maybe even become fatal. Many cases of dysthymia result in major depression; up to 17 percent of untreated depressions end in suicide.

Subtle and easy to miss, dysthymia becomes a way of life. And most people don't do anything about. *Don't be one of them.*

If you do nothing, you may be doomed to years washed out in a monotone of bleakness. Chances are, you will slow down, have less energy and little motivation to do much of anything and so will spend more time alone, brooding and isolated from others. The more people brood and isolate themselves, the less energy or motivation they tend to have to do anything about it.

Rita, a 28-year-old doctoral candidate, put all her energies into work and school. But she saw herself as a fake and a failure. "I couldn't escape this sense of gloom and emptiness. All I wanted to do was to give up. I felt depressed no matter what I did."

But if you *can* recognize that you're glum and negative, you're halfway there. Now, you have a chance to break your patterns.

"Your way of explaining events to yourself determines how helpless you can become, or how energized, when you encounter the everyday setbacks as well as momentous defeats."

—Martin Seligman, *Learned Optimism*

If dysthymia is only mild, why bother?

For the sake of your
  Enthusiasm
    Sense of hope
      Sense of well-being
        Sense of purpose
          Your ability to show and receive love

Do you really enjoy going through life at half-speed, half-heartedly?

The Revolution in Mental Health

Dysthymia is currently recognized as the epidemic common cold of mental health. But unlike high blood pressure or diabetes, dysthymia has been largely unrecognized and undertreated. Dysthymia is now being taken seriously as a highly treatable condition because new ways of viewing chronic mild depression are revolutionizing treatment, with strategies to use your thoughts to manage moods, to develop coping skills, and to improve relationships and with a new generation of antidepressants for those who need them. Researchers now know that at least 80 percent of those who seek appropriate help experience dramatic relief within six months.

Many studies also suggest that exercise, relaxation methods, and perhaps even dietary supplements, particularly St. John's wort, can have powerful influences on relieving dysthymia. Because dysthymia is fairly mild compared with major depression, these therapies can make a real difference. Researchers are also excited about new insights into brain function and how the differences between "depressed" and "never depressed" brains can be identified. Using biofeedback methods, they hope to be able to learn how to change brain patterns to function more as "never depressed," in the same way that biofeedback can teach us how to influence some parts of the nervous system that we don't normally control (pulse, breathing, heart rate, temperature, etc.).

COPING STRATEGIES AND SKILLS

Chronic mild depression can be relieved by learning strategies that help you to leave the past behind and cope more effectively with the setbacks and interpersonal difficulties of everyday life. These types of skills are taught in cognitive-behavioral and interpersonal styles of psychotherapy and can both prevent the onset and relieve the problems of dysthymia and depression.

Cognitive-behavioral skills focus on how recognizing negative and distorted thinking patterns can help to turn around a downward spiral of pessimism. Research has repeatedly proven that the style you use to frame your thoughts dramatically influences how you feel and your resulting moods. It is also clear that how you explain life's setbacks and disappointments to yourself can make all the difference between whether you are in good moods or bad moods most of the time.

"If we see things as negative, we are likely to feel negative and behave in a negative way."

—Aaron T. Beck, professor emeritus of psychiatry, University of Pennsylvania, and the father of cognitive therapy

---

If you exaggerate how bad this or that was, for example, see the world as black or white, tell yourself you're not good enough, or that you blew it, that kind of pessimism will dampen your moods and sour your relationships. It may also persist and get worse if just left unattended. Negative ways of thinking are stressful, and researchers are finding that such thoughts and moods also can have a profound influence on your brain's biochemistry over time, making you ever more likely to become more depressed in the future.

"If you want to feel better, you must realize that your thoughts and attitudes—not external events—create your feelings."

—David Burns, *Feeling Good*

Interpersonal therapy skills focus on how interpersonal problems can cause unhappiness and how to apply interpersonal skills and problem-solving strategies to improve relationships. This therapy looks at how loss (grief), difficult relationships, and transitions cause chronic stress and how problems with social skills often result in social isolation. By clarifying your goals and expectations, you can shift your attention away from the past to the present and develop new activities and relationships. After all—the past is gone, the future hasn't happened, and all we have control of is what we do with the present.

MEDICATIONS

Although the cognitive strategies mentioned above can help anyone live a more balanced life by teaching your inner voice to be constructive instead of destructive, sometimes the brain's biochemistry is so imbalanced that medication is helpful to normalize the brain and allow it to be "receptive" again. The brain perhaps could be thought of as a powerful machine that after a period of prolonged operation under demanding circumstances needs to be overhauled before it can respond properly to a new set of challenges. In this analogy, antidepressants "tune up" the brain's stress responses.

With new understandings of how brain chemistry affects mood and behavior, researchers have developed safer antidepressants that are helpful for both mild and severe depressions. The effectiveness of the medications may increase even more when used in conjunction with the cognitive strategies that teach you how to stop viewing life's setbacks as "personal, permanent, and pervasive," observes Martin Seligman, one of the leading researchers in cognitive psychotherapy and depression.

Some experts are beginning to embrace the value of various long-neglected alternative treatments, including stress management (meditation, relaxation, massage, biofeedback), physical exercise, acupuncture, and other mind/body therapies, in reducing depressive (and anxious) symptoms.

What Can You Do?

The first step for getting out of the gray zone where feeling good is rare and temporary is to recognize you're stuck there. Eking out a life cast in pessimism will only perpetuate your bad moods and promote low productivity and poor health. By recognizing you have a problem, you are empowered to try to do something about it.

- Learn to identify the signs of mild depression and dysthymia, not only in yourself but in those you love. Be particularly watchful in children, adolescents, and elderly persons, as well as those who live with chronic stress; these populations are at particularly high risk. (See chapters 4, 11, 13.)
- Take advantage of the principles used in the styles of psychotherapy that have been proven to help depression. They can help you change pessimistic, self-defeating explanatory patterns of thinking into constructive and healthy styles of thinking, promote positive action, and enhance interpersonal relationships. (See chapter 5.)
- Understand what medications can and can't do. (See chapter 7.)
- Explore alternative ways that often help to relieve dysthymia, including exercise, self-help groups, and herbal supplements. (See chapters 8, 9, and 10.)

Dysthymia is not a reflection of any kind of shortcoming. It has nothing to do with not having enough inner strength or fortitude. These kinds of attitudes have created a stigma that implies that admitting to dysthymia or depression is admitting to a character flaw.

In fact, recognizing that you have a problem and taking action to do something about it is not only courageous but responsible. Whether you feel like it or not, just making the attempt can make a difference, as we'll see in subsequent chapters.

For if you always do what you've always done, you'll always get what you've always gotten.

And if that's not enough motivation, then consider this: Once someone is treated appropriately for dysthymia, that person's risk of having a recurrence is no greater than someone who's never had dysthymia. In other words, once you get better, you stay better.

If you want to read about how to help yourself right away, skip the next few chapters and go directly to chapter 5.

2

♦ ♦ ♦

The Spectrum of Dysthymia
and Depression

How weary, stale, flat, and unprofitable
seem to me all the uses of this world!

—William Shakespeare, *Hamlet*

Before we look at the causes of dysthymia and how to relieve a chronic
blue mood, let's first see what good mental health looks like and then
look at the spectrum of depression—from minor depression to dysthymia and major depression.

Feeling Good and Mental Health

If you are mentally healthy and well balanced, on most days you feel
pretty good. You're more often in a good mood than not, have a sense of
well-being, and feel pretty much in control of life. You're generally productive, enjoy fulfilling relationships with others, and are somewhat resilient when life smacks you in the face with a loss or setback. You're
relatively confident and competent, and pursue various interests with a
sense of purpose.

Another barometer of mental well-being is your "emotional intelligence,"
which some experts say is more critical to life success than one's IQ.

We all encounter pain and setbacks. But how you respond to adversity and loss and how you explain adverse external events to yourself
make the difference between an upbeat positive outlook and the slip-
pery slope down toward pessimism.

Signs of mental well-being are that you

Accept yourself, the good and the bad

Maintain close, positive and trusting interpersonal relationships

Feel relatively in control of your life, able to make decisions and resist peer pressure

Recognize purpose in life: follow a sense of direction toward general goals

Pursue areas of personal growth to continue growing and understanding yourself and life better

You are emotionally intelligent if you

Can motivate yourself

Keep trying despite frustration

Despite your feelings, don't act them out with inappropriate behavior (tantrums, rage)

Can postpone gratification, knowing that it's better for you to do something else first

Can empathize with another person's point of view

Can keep distress in perspective, without catastrophizing

Can hope

—based on Daniel Goleman, *Emotional Intelligence*

Next, we'll look at the various shades of depressions. As you try to figure out where you fit in, remember that you are not the diagnosis (discussed in more detail in the next chapter). That is, the diagnosis is based on symptoms and the behaviors they trigger. The diagnosis is important in that it informs treatment: it's not who you are.

Minor Depression

We all have bad moods and blue days—life can be tough with disappointments, deaths, periods of self-doubt, negativity, and fatigue when you lose your energy and motivation. But bad moods that persist chip away at your sense of hope and optimism, corrode your self-esteem, and make it harder to bounce back.

Minor depression*
Episodes of a relatively persistent depressed mood that last at least two weeks.

Also, at least one but not more than five of these symptoms:
    Poor appetite
    Sleep difficulty
    Problems concentrating
    Agitation
    Fatigue
    Loss of energy
    Loss of self-esteem
    Guilt, worthlessness

Symptoms must be severe enough to cause distress and to interfere with normal activity.

*also called subsyndromal depression or SSD

The next figure shows a person who is usually in a normal mood but experiences a minor depression.

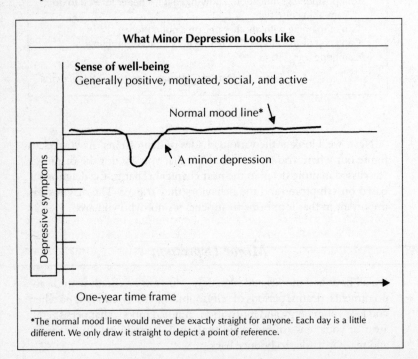

What Minor Depression Looks Like

Sense of well-being
Generally positive, motivated, social, and active

Normal mood line*

A minor depression

Depressive symptoms

One-year time frame

*The normal mood line would never be exactly straight for anyone. Each day is a little different. We only draw it straight to depict a point of reference.

Milder than depression and too brief to be dysthymia, minor depressions usually don't catch the attention of loved ones or family doctors, but they are distressing and compromise life in a clearly negative way.

Although a minor depression may seem like no big deal, it is a significant risk factor for dysthymia and major depression:

- Almost 30 percent young adults with minor depression will have a major depression within 15 years.
- Minor depression also alters the course of subsequent bouts of major depression. Of those who suffer a major depression, one-half will never fully recover (often because alcohol and drug use interfere with treatment) but will be left with a lingering minor depression.
- With a minor depression, you are far more likely to have problems sleeping and concentrating, to feel run down, and to be prone to gain weight than people with one or no depressive symptoms.

Experts don't want to dissect every blue mood and usually wouldn't recommend an antidepressant at this point on the depression spectrum—such depressions are mild and temporary, haven't been studied much, and are overshadowed by major depressions. Also, minor depression varies widely. Nevertheless, the coping skills in chapter 5 have the potential to prevent a mild depression from getting worse.

How common is minor depression? Estimates vary, but researchers generally agree that from 3 to 9 percent of Americans (about 8 to 23 million people) experience minor depression sometime during their lives.

When a Crisis Causes Distress

Some periods of low mood are normal due to a crisis. When something horrible happens—someone you love dies, you divorce, you lose your job, you have a serious illness—it's normal to feel sad and depressed and to cry or experience other symptoms that are the same as those of depression and dysthymia (see Depression vs. Dysthymia chart, p. 21). It's normal for these symptoms to persist for up to about three months after such an event and up to a year for bereavement. These depressive symptoms, however, aren't considered a minor or major depression, but "uncomplicated bereavement" (i.e., grief) or, if treatment is sought for something other than grief, an "adjustment disorder with depressive symptoms," according to the American Psychiatric Association's source book of psychiatric disorders—the *DSM-IV* (short for *Diagnostic and Statistical Manual of Mental Disorders, Fourth Edition*). There is nothing unusual, wrong, or unhealthy about these responses to adversity. We all experience them as they are part of human nature. It is only if the symptoms become severe (intense and frequent) and persist that normal sadness begins to transform into depression.

The strategies discussed in this book are very relevant to this type of depression as well.

Dysthymia

If the symptoms last for at least two years, however, and cast shadows over most days but do not become severe, it's considered dysthymia, according to the *DSM-IV.*

> "Mild depression (dysthymia) is a gradual and sometimes permanent thing that undermines people the way rust weakens iron. It is too much grief at too slight a cause, pain that takes over from the other emotions and crowds them out."
>
> —Andrew Solomon, *The Noonday Demon*

Dysthymia is disabling because it gnaws at you every day, wearing away at your quality of life. It hovers and hangs for so long, often decades, that you may just come to accept your pessimistic view as interwoven into your personality. But in fact, this negative view on life is how you are responding. It's not "you," not who you are—it's just how you respond. Not a personality trait, dsythymia is a mood disorder that drains your energy and dampens your mood. You can still manage to go to work and do what needs to be done, but you are run down, apathetic, negative, passive, and self-loathing. That makes it harder and harder to function well at home, school, or work. You're unhappy and dissatisfied whether good things happen or not. Going through the motions of daily living, day in and day out, life comes to feel like a chore, a struggle, a grim grind of quiet desperation. Everything is an effort with very little positive payoff.

The figure appearing on page 20 diagrams how the moods of a person with dysthymia might appear.

Relatively Speaking: The Severity of Depressions

0	1	2	3	4	5	6	7	8	9	10
Generally happy, optimistic, hopeful, active	**Minor Depression** (Episodic) Apathetic Lethargic Not as interested in hobbies and activities Often feels down, blue, blah Doesn't feel like doing things but generally does them anyway			**Mild Depression (If chronic = Dysthymia)** (Symptoms from minor depression but more intense) Occasionally: Gets choked up a lot, cries Tired Anxious Changes in eating Some changes in sleeping patterns Difficulty concentrating Less interest in sex, activities Low frustration level Feelings of hopelessness Doesn't feel like doing things and sometimes won't do them (mild functional impairment)			**Major Depression** (Symptoms from moderate depression become more frequent and intense) Depressed all the time; feels system is shut down Can't make decisions, never wants to do things Thinks about suicide Frequently (daily): Gets choked up a lot, cries Tired Anxious Changes in eating Some changes in sleeping patterns Difficulty concentrating Less interest in sex, activities Low frustration level Feelings of hopelessness Doesn't feel like doing things and often won't do them (marked functional impairment)			

0–10 scale is the spectrum of depression: 0 indicates no depression; 10 indicates a severe depression.

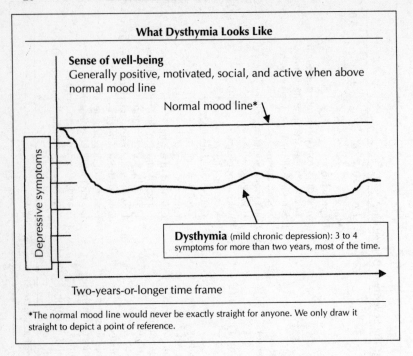

What Dysthymia Looks Like

Sense of well-being
Generally positive, motivated, social, and active when above normal mood line

Normal mood line*

Depressive symptoms

Dysthymia (mild chronic depression): 3 to 4 symptoms for more than two years, most of the time.

Two-years-or-longer time frame

*The normal mood line would never be exactly straight for anyone. We only draw it straight to depict a point of reference.

Although the symptoms of dysthymia are mild to moderate in intensity, experts consider the condition severe because it is chronic.

Major Depression

If you feel down most of the time or rarely feel pleasure and joy and also suffer from at least four other symptoms, you may have a major depression, according to the *DSM-IV. If so, you should see a physician or mental health professional immediately, especially if you harbor thoughts of suicide.* With a major depression, you may not even be able to function; though many people manage to drag themselves through the day, they are certainly nowhere near their peak performance. Helplessness, hopelessness, sleeping and eating problems, crying, low self-image, and a negative attitude are typical symptoms. Depressed people feel as though life is a monotonous, oppressive burden and may not care if they live or die.

This chart compares the symptoms of depression with dysthymia, according to the *DSM-IV.*

Depression	vs.	Dysthymia
You feel either A and/or B and four other symptoms for at least two weeks.		You feel A for at least two years and two other symptoms while depressed.
A. Depressed mood most of the day on most days. (In children and adolescents, this may be irritability instead.)		A. Depressed mood most of the day on most days for at least two years. (In children and adolescents, this may be irritability instead.)
B. Rarely feel pleasure or joy.		Feelings of hopelessness.
Significant weight gain or loss.		Significant weight gain or loss.
Can't sleep or sleep too much, on most days.		Can't sleep or sleep too much, on most days.
Almost always feel tired and low energy.		Almost always feel tired and low energy.
Difficulty concentrating or making decisions almost all the time.		Difficulty concentrating or making decisions.
Feel guilt or worthlessness nearly all the time.		Low self-esteem.
Noticeably agitated or passive and slowed down.		
Think frequently about death and/or suicide.		

As you can see, dysthymia and depression share many symptoms. What differentiates the two are primarily the intensity, frequency, and duration of the symptoms. The chart below highlights these differences.

Comparing Dysthymia and Major Depression		
	Dysthymia	Major Depression
Onset	Very gradually	Quite suddenly
Symptoms	Mostly cognitive, social, and motivational; functional ones may be present	Functional symptoms usually present: eating, sleeping, agitated or passive
Normal moods	Last up to 2 months	Rare
Number of symptoms	At least 2	At least 5
Length of symptoms	At least 2 years	At least 2 weeks
Intensity of symptoms	Mild to moderate	Mild to severe
Pattern of symptoms	Symptoms come and go	Symptoms cluster together into episodes
Noticeable to family or friends	Not very noticeable	Quite noticeable

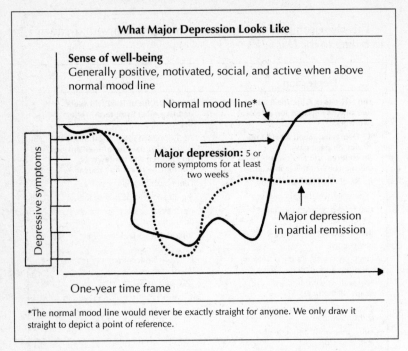

What Major Depression Looks Like

Sense of well-being
Generally positive, motivated, social, and active when above normal mood line

Normal mood line*

Depressive symptoms

Major depression: 5 or more symptoms for at least two weeks

Major depression in partial remission

One-year time frame

*The normal mood line would never be exactly straight for anyone. We only draw it straight to depict a point of reference.

Major depression can be incapacitating: despair, doom, and thoughts of death can darken every single day. These sufferers of depression say it best:

> "In depression, the meaninglessness of every enterprise and every emotion, the meaninglessness of life itself, becomes self-evident. The only feeling left in this loveless state is insignificance. . . . If one imagines a soul of iron that weathers with grief and rusts with mild depression, then major depression is the startling collapse of a whole structure."
>
> —Andrew Solomon, *The Noonday Demon*

> "I am now the most miserable man living. If what I feel were equally distributed to the whole human family, there would be not one cheerful face on earth. Whether I shall ever be better, I cannot tell. I awfully forebode I shall not. To remain as I am is impossible. I must die or be better it appears to me."
>
> —Abraham Lincoln, in a letter to John T. Stuart, his first law partner, January 23, 1841

"Every day I would wake, after usually a very troubled sleep with a sense of despair. It got worse and resolved itself into this unfocused pain, which I found almost unbearable. . . . The pain grew and grew and I began to experience suicidal thoughts. I realized that life for me was at a desperate impasse. . . . One particular night in the fall, following months of this seizure of depression, suicide thoughts were overwhelming me. That night, I lost myself in a kind of psychosis. There was an absolute incoherence in my behavior and my thoughts. I began to get frantic; I was in a state of semi-delirium."

—William Styron, author of *Sophie's Choice*, in an interview with the organization Families for Depression Awareness: http://www.familyaware.org

Unfortunately, if you suffer from major depression, you may not fully recover unless you get treatment. If you only partially recover, you will likely move from a major depression to a milder limbo state that is called a major depression in partial remission. If a partial remission persists for two years or longer, it is virtually indistinguishable from dysthymia.

Double Depression

When a person with dysthymia develops a major depressive episode (which is quite common), both conditions are diagnosed. The clinical term for this type of chronic depression is double depression.

The figure on page 24 shows how a double depression wobbles between dysthymia and major depression.

Before we go into the gritty details of how these conditions are diagnosed, let's explore how feelings of dissatisfaction, sadness, and grieving can be distinguished from dysthymic symptoms, especially when they aren't severe or chronic.

Dysthymia Is Not Dysphoria

Dysphoria is a fancy word for a bad mood; it's usually a passing mood of general dissatisfaction, restlessness, depression, anxiety, or irritability. Passing dysphoria is a normal response to frustration, setbacks, or other losses. Feelings of sadness and sorrow are expected reactions to

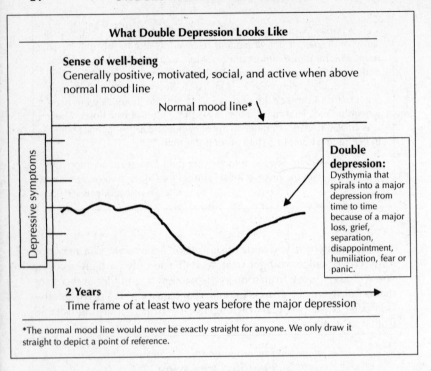

What Double Depression Looks Like

Sense of well-being
Generally positive, motivated, social, and active when above normal mood line

Normal mood line*

Depressive symptoms

Double depression: Dysthymia that spirals into a major depression from time to time because of a major loss, grief, separation, disappointment, humiliation, fear or panic.

2 Years
Time frame of at least two years before the major depression

*The normal mood line would never be exactly straight for anyone. We only draw it straight to depict a point of reference.

life's many losses and disappointments; virtually everyone feels dysphoric from time to time. Dysphoria becomes a potential problem if it spirals into a minor or major depression. Dysphoria is very common—as many as 1 in 5 people, psychologists estimate, are unhappy at any given time—but chronic feelings of dysphoria also can turn into dysthymia. The strategies used in this book can also help to dissipate dysphoria.

Dysthymia Is Not Grief

Grief—mourning the death of a loved one—looks like depression, except grief is normally short-lived (usually three to six months, sometimes up to a year) and it usually is a fully appropriate reaction to loss. If you can love, you can grieve. Some mental health experts distinguish between grief (loss by death) from emotional reactions to other kinds of loss, although the experiences are virtually identical. Loss is a theme that threads itself throughout the human condition. How you weather the storms of loss has a profound role in whether you are resilient and adaptable and progress through the normal stages of loss and grief or are prone to slipping into dysthymia or depression.

> "These losses are a part of life—universal, unavoidable, inexorable. And these losses are necessary because we grow by losing and leaving and letting go.
>
> "In the course of our life we leave and are left and let go of much that we love. Losing is the price we pay for living. It is also the source of much of our growth and gain. . . . opportunities for creative transformations. . . .
>
> "For we cannot deeply love anything without becoming vulnerable to loss. "
>
> —Judith Viorst, *Necessary Losses*

You can grieve for other kinds of losses, such as the loss of a job, a child that marries and moves away, the selling of a house in which you spent happy decades, and so on. Everyone experiences losses, but it is how you respond to your losses that determines if you are mentally healthy or moving into the bleak depressive zone of sadness and despair.

> "Grief is depression in proportion to circumstance; depression is grief out of proportion to circumstance."
>
> —Andrew Solomon, *The Noonday Demon*

Sadness is fine just as it is—it is honest and loving, genuine and real. You may be in such pain that you don't notice if the sadness begins to color your world and you come to view the world pessimistically. Loss is undeniably sad, but what you tell yourself is what turns sad into bad. If we lament, "This shouldn't happen to me" and whine to yourself "Why me?" you not only get stuck in a rut but increasingly negative.

As Judith Viorst writes in *Necessary Losses:* "Our losses include not only our separations and departures from those we love, but our conscious and unconscious losses of romantic dreams, impossible expectations, illusions of freedom and power, illusions of safety—the loss of our own younger self, the self that thought it always would be unwrinkled and invulnerable and immortal."

Losses are unavoidable but they are universal. They happen to everyone; they're not unique to you. They are a part of life, not apart from life. What sets up the triggers for a depressive point of view is our *reaction* to loss. If we are negative and pessimistic, we turn genuine grief that is honest and human into a depression that is self-defeating and a monster.

How we deal with loss—healthfully

The normal healthy response, even in the worst of circumstances, is to work through the stages of loss, not necessarily in this order and with many fits and starts:

- Shock, numbness, disbelief, incomprehension
- Weeping, suffer the rawness of deep, fresh pain
- Anger, at the world, at yourself, at God
- Guilt: Ask yourself what you could have done, blame yourself for what you should have done
- Bargaining: "If only it could have been . . . If only I'd done that." Replay the loss and doubt yourself
- Depression, despair
- Acceptance: Life has to go on despite the profound loss, although anniversaries of renewed tears are normal
- Adaptation

Through the adaptation comes a burst of self-growth.

Even though it's among the hardest things we ever have to do, we must stop ourselves from ruminating over what happened and trying to control it (which will lead to depression). We need to accept the sadness although it hurts so much and we don't like doing it. We need to accept the loss as reality and focus instead on what to do next. (See chapter 5.)

"Let it be."

—Paul McCartney

There is no set timetable for recovering from loss, but the more you can keep track of the stage you are in, the more you will be able to understand that, "All things must pass."

Dysthymia Is Not Loneliness

Many people with dysthymia feel lonely and isolated from others. If your loneliness distresses you or impairs your functioning, then the loneliness may develop into dysthymia.

Many grief experts use the same kind of constructive thinking (cognitive) strategies, described in chapter 5, to prevent loneliness from turning into a mood disorder.

Dysthymia Is Not Necessarily Sadness

As noted in the previous chapter, sometimes depression surfaces without sadness. Many symptoms of dysthymia don't resemble sadness. These include a lack of interest in things you used to enjoy, apathy, feeling numb emotionally, irritability, fatigue, negativity, poor self-esteem, self-criticism, lack of confidence, loss of sexual desire or appetite, social withdrawal, lack of motivation, and guilt (although sadness may still be at the root of these symptoms). You can also be sad and not depressed. Sadness is a normal and healthy reaction to certain events and sadness comes and goes. Depression comes and stays—an uninvited guest that unknowingly moves in and takes over your home.

On the Dark Side	
Passing mood/states that may briefly interrupt normal mood	
Dysphoria	Short-lived moods of general dissatisfaction
Loneliness	Doesn't necessarily cause distress or dysfunction
Sadness	Short-lived, expected and normal response to grief
Types of Depression from mild to severe	**Symptoms**
Adjustment disorder with depressive mood	A normal reaction to major life stressors.
Minor Depression	Several depressive symptoms that last a few weeks or more
Dysthymia	Mild depressive symptoms that are chronic (at least two years)
Major Depression	Severe depressed mood or loss of interest with at least 4 other symptoms for at least 2 weeks, but can persist for years.

Other Types of Depression

Although the focus of this book is dysthymia, it's important to understand how dysthymia relates to other types of depression.

ATYPICAL DEPRESSION

Some people with depression can brighten up and feel better temporarily when something good happens, a feature called *mood reactivity*. When mood reactivity is accompanied by symptoms such as overeating or oversleeping, the term atypical depression may be used. Historically, the term *atypical* was used because insomnia and weight loss were considered more classic (or typical) symptoms of depression. This term is outdated because we know now that oversleeping and overeating are actually fairly common symptoms in younger people who become depressed. Another feature of an atypical depression is being highly sensitive to rejection.

Although we know atypical depression is four times more common in women than in men, getting a handle on exactly how many people experience this type of depression is difficult. Estimates indicate that somewhere between 15 and 40 percent of those diagnosed with a major depression or dysthymia also experience features of atypical depression.

And although their features are different, atypical depression has similar causes to and is treated the same as dysthymia or depression.

SEASONAL AFFECTIVE DISORDER

Seasonal affective disorder (SAD) is recurrent depression that occurs during the fall or winter but passes in the spring or summer. During the winter, if you have SAD, you will feel tired and you may want to overeat (particularly carbohydrates) and oversleep. Again, the cognitive and behavioral skills discussed later can help someone suffering from SAD (as well as anyone, in fact). Therapists also recommend exposure to plenty of bright, full-spectrum lighting, such as from desktop light panels specially designed to relieve SAD. Many people with SAD also experience short-lived natural "highs" (or hypomanias) in the spring or summer.

SAD is prevalent in less than 1 percent of the adult population of the United States and Asia, and up to 3 percent in Canada and Europe. About 75 percent of all people who experience depression will suffer at least one recurrence in the subsequent ten years: of those who do, about 15 percent experience the fall and winter depression pattern characteristic of SAD.

PREMENSTRUAL DYSPHORIC DISORDER

If you have monthly depressions that correspond with your menstrual cycle, you might have premenstrual dysphoric disorder (PDD or

PMDD; also called late-luteal dysphoric disorder). Usually, you start experiencing at least five depression symptoms during most periods, starting a week or so before menstruation and ending after you stop bleeding.

Estimates for the prevalence of PDD range from 3 to 8 percent of women in their reproductive years.

POSTPARTUM DEPRESSION

Some pregnant women and women just after childbirth are overwhelmed with irritability, anxiety, moodiness, loss of self-esteem, crying jags, and other symptoms of depression. Known as postpartum depression, this condition should be distinguished from the "baby blues," a mild slump in mood that lasts only a few days or weeks. All women undergo huge hormonal upheavals during this time and some may feel overwhelmed by the new responsibilities of motherhood. However, women experiencing depression after birth should discuss it with their doctors, as treatment is often required.

About 10 to 15 percent of women experience postpartum depression after the birth of a child.

MAJOR DEPRESSION WITH PSYCHOTIC FEATURES

It is almost never normal to hallucinate. Some people develop strong fixed beliefs about past sins, current illness, or guilt that cannot be refuted by facts; these are called delusions. Together, delusions and hallucinations are called psychotic features.

Unlike schizophrenia or mania, relatively few—5 to 10 percent—of people with major depression have psychotic features.

Dysthymia is never characterized by these features.

Now that we have made some distinctions among the various forms of depression, let's look more closely at how dysthymia is diagnosed, its causes, and its risk factors.

3

◆ ◆ ◆

How Dysthymia Is Diagnosed

I have secluded myself
From society;
And yet I never meant
Any such thing.
I have made a captive of myself
And put me into a dungeon,
And now I cannot find the key
To let myself out.

—Nathaniel Hawthorne, in a letter to poet
Henry Wadsworth Longfellow in 1837

Having read chapter 2, you know whether you might be dysthymic or suffering from another form of depression, and that we recommend that you consult a physician or mental health professional promptly.

If you think you might be dysthymic, we have two other choices for you. Skip immediately to chapters 5 to 10 for strategies to relieve the symptoms of dysthymia and prevent relapse. Or, review this chapter to learn how dysthymia is diagnosed. But don't get caught up in the technicalities of your diagnosis. The most important part of understanding a diagnosis is that it informs treatment.

Has Your Good Cheer
Turned Blue?

Do you find that you no longer feel "good" on most days? That you're more often in a bad mood, have lost a sense of purpose in your life, or are having trouble with your family or friends? As dysthymia takes its smoldering course, it would be sapping your energy and making it harder and harder to get through the day with its many demands. You might not have noticed that numerous dysthymic symptoms have crept into your life and are staying longer and longer. So, ask yourself:

- Am I pessimistic, passive, less decisive, having trouble concentrating, seeing friends less often, and down on myself?
- Do I still feel joy and love doing certain things?
- Do I often behave in a negative, critical, or jealous manner?
- Do people respond differently to me than in the past?

SELF-REPORT TESTS

Here is one of the widely used depression inventory self-tests to determine where you might fall on the spectrum of depression.

Depression Test

(adapted from the Center for Epidemiological Studies [CES-D], National Institute of Mental Health)

Below is a list of the ways you might have felt or behaved. How often have you felt this way during the past week?

	During the Past Week			
	Rarely or none of the time (less than 1 day)	Some or a little of the time (1–2 days)	Occasionally or a moderate amount of the time (3–4 days)	Most or all of the time (5–7 days)
1. I was bothered by things that usually don't bother me.	☐	☐	☐	☐
2. I did not feel like eating; my appetite was poor.	☐	☐	☐	☐
3. I felt that I could not shake off the blues even with help from my family or friends.	☐	☐	☐	☐
4. I felt I was not as good as other people.	☐	☐	☐	☐
5. I had trouble keeping my mind on what I was doing.	☐	☐	☐	☐
6. I felt depressed.	☐	☐	☐	☐
7. I felt that everything I did was an effort.	☐	☐	☐	☐
8. I felt unhopeful about the future.	☐	☐	☐	☐
9. I thought my life had been a failure.	☐	☐	☐	☐

(continues)

Depression Test (*continued*)

During the Past Week

	Rarely or none of the time (less than 1 day)	Some or a little of the time (1–2 days)	Occasionally or a moderate amount of the time (3–4 days)	Most or all of the time (5–7 days)
10. I felt fearful.	☐	☐	☐	☐
11. My sleep was restless.	☐	☐	☐	☐
12. I was unhappy.	☐	☐	☐	☐
13. I talked less than usual.	☐	☐	☐	☐
14. I felt lonely.	☐	☐	☐	☐
15. People were unfriendly.	☐	☐	☐	☐
16. I did not enjoy life.	☐	☐	☐	☐
17. I had crying spells.	☐	☐	☐	☐
18. I felt sad.	☐	☐	☐	☐
19. I felt that people dislike me.	☐	☐	☐	☐
20. I could not get going.	☐	☐	☐	☐

SCORING: Zero for answers in the first column, 1 for answers in the second column, 2 for answers in the third column, 3 for answers in the fourth column. Possible range of scores is zero to 60, with the higher scores indicating the presence of more symptoms.

0–5: Not depressed

6–9 : Subthreshold depression

10–15: Mildly depressed (dysthymic if has persisted for 2 years; 1 year for children and teens)

16–24: Moderately depressed

over 24: May be severely depressed

We strongly recommend that you see a physician or mental health professional if you scored over 15.

Although this test and other depression inventories are useful to prescreen yourself, a mental health specialist—a psychiatrist, psychologist, psychiatric nurse, or clinical social worker—is best trained to diagnose dysthymia and other forms of depression. Various screening tests are used, including the Beck Depression Inventory, Hamilton Rating Scale, Zung Depression Inventory, Burns Depression Checklist, and the Cornell Dysthymia Rating Scale. In addition to using one of these questionnaires, a specialist would conduct a formal mental status evaluation to look for changes in your thought patterns, feelings, behaviors, as well as in your eating and sleeping habits to glean insight into what's contributing to your dysthymic condition. Using your score on the test and taking into account how often you answer yes to questions such as: Do you often feel irritable? Are you indecisive? Have your eating or sleeping patterns changed recently?, which might signal changes in your mental health, the clinician would make a diagnosis.

CHANGES WITH DYSTHYMIA

Changes in Feelings

- Low self-esteem (more than any other symptom, people with dysthymia report declining self-esteem the most frequently)
- Sad for no apparent reason
- Little pleasure from activities you used to enjoy
- Irritable
- Lack motivation
- Apathetic
- Pessimistic or less hopeful than in the past
- Feel more helpless about making changes or solving problems

Changes in Thinking

- Poor concentration
- Short-term memory problems
- Indecision
- Ruminations and worries
- Suicidal or morbid thoughts

Changes in Behavior

- Missing deadlines, taking frequent sick days
- Loss of appetite or overeating
- Restlessness or being slowed down
- Insomnia or oversleeping

Alison has never failed in school or been fired from a job, but neither has she ever seemed to live up to her potential. She's always been underemployed and most of her relationships have fizzled out within a few months. She has little self-confidence and, as a result, doesn't seek out friends or jobs that are more rewarding.

Typical profile of a person with dysthymia

In general, researchers note that people living with dysthymia tend to be

- Loyal workers but underachievers
- Underemployed (hold jobs below their abilities)
- Somewhat more rigid about changes
- Poor at coping skills
- Timid, socially withdrawn, and rarely take risks or are domineering
- Sleeping too much
- Unmarried or divorced; if married, the relationship is often dead-locked
- Afflicted with other medical problems
- Afflicted with other mental health problems, especially major depression, anxiety disorders (especially panic disorder), substance abuse, and probably borderline personality disorder

---

Physical Problems

Most people living with dysthymia don't recognize their symptoms as chronic mild depression but go to their doctors complaining of headaches, fatigue, and stomach problems—the same symptoms linked to stress. People from some cultures are much less likely to report mood-related symptoms but instead report their physical symptoms, such as chronic fatigue, sluggishness, feeling "slowed down" or run down, stress, headaches, weakness, aches and pains, including backache, and gastrointestinal problems.

SEEING THE FAMILY DOCTOR

If you experience several of the symptoms discussed above and have been for some time, you could go either to a psychotherapist or to a physician. If you are taking medications, have a chronic illness or suspect an illness, it probably would be best to go first to a physician. Getting a complete physical is important to rule out the possibility that a physical illness or medication, other mental disorder, or the challenges of living with a chronic illness or physical disability are the cause of your depressed mood. Be sure to mention drug, alcohol, and cigarette use as well. Failed attempts to quit these habits also can trigger depressive symptoms. Also, mention any supplements or vitamins you take on a regular basis. If you don't mention depressive symptoms when you see your doctor, the chances are only 1 out of 4 that your doctor will detect them, so be sure to speak up.

RULING OUT MEDICAL ILLNESSES

One out of three people who have medical conditions experience significant depressive symptoms, reports the National Institute of Mental Health. This is largely because being sick can get you down. But many illnesses also can cause depression directly, including low thyroid (hypothyroidism). Hypothyroidism can cause depressed mood, loss of interest, loss of pleasure, weight gain, sleep and concentration problems, chronic fatigue, and sluggishness that are indistinguishable from the symptoms of dysthymia. Low thyroid is more common among women and may also result in people being less responsive to psychotherapy or antidepressants.

Endocrine disorders, such as Cushing's disease, Addison's disease, and diabetes (note: half of the 15 million diabetics in this country don't know they have diabetes), can cause weight loss, fatigue, and sleep problems, all typical depressive symptoms. Central nervous system disorders (Parkinson's disease, brain tumor, brain aneurysm, stroke, lupus, transient ischemic attacks, and dementia) may trigger apathy, poor concentration, and memory loss. Also, nutritional deficiencies (specifically folate, vitamin B-12, and niacin), chronic high blood pressure, migraines, hypoglycemia, lead poisoning, allergies, endometriosis, infectious diseases (mononucleosis, hepatitis, encephalitis, urinary tract infections, meningitis, and bacterial infection) are also sometimes implicated in depression. Less common medical disorders that cause depressive symptoms include dehydration, uremia, hypoxia, and Wilson's disease. Some cancers also may have directly depressing effects on brain function, even before a malignancy is detected.

Sometimes, treating the underlying condition will relieve depressive symptoms. Sometimes conventional antidepressant treatments are needed as well.

RULING OUT MEDICATIONS

Many medications can trigger depressive symptoms, such as pain relievers prescribed for arthritis, medications used to lower cholesterol and high blood pressure, some heart disease drugs and medications that are prescribed for asthma. Some steroids, tranquilizers, sedatives, and over-the-counter diet and sleeping pills can cause depressive symptoms as well. Up to 10 percent of women who take birth control pills will experience an increase in depressive symptoms. This relationship can be overlooked because many people don't think of contraceptives as medication.

Some medications that can provoke depressive symptoms

ACTH (corticotropin)
acyclovir (Zovirax)
alpha-methyldopa
amantadine
amphetamines
anabolic steroids
antibiotics (such as tetracycline, ampicillin, streptomycin)
anticonvulsants
antineoplastic (cancer fighting) drugs
asparaginase (Elspar)
baclofen (Lioresal)
barbiturates (such as Valium)
benzodiazepines (when abused)
beta-adrenergic blockers or beta-blocking drugs (such as Inderal, Lopressor)
birth control pills
bromocriptine (Parlodel)
calcium-channel blockers
captopril (Capoten)
carbazepine
chloral hydrate
chlorpromazine (Thorazine)
cimetidine (Tagamet)
clonidine (Catapres)
cocaine (withdrawal)
corticosteroids
cycloserine (Seromycin)
dapsone
diazepam (Valium)
digitalis
disopyramide (Norpace)
disulfiram (Antabuse)
Estrogens and progesterones (any estrogen replacement therapies)
Ethambutol
Fluoroquinolone antibiotics
Flurazepam (Dalmane)
Glucocorticoids
Guanethidine
Haloperidol (Haldol)
Histamine H2-receptor antagonists
HMG-CoA reductase inhibitors (statins)

Hydralazine (Apresazide)
Ibuprofen (Advil, Nuprin, Motrin)
Indapamide
indomethacin
Interferon alfa (Roferon-A)
Isotretinoin (Accutane)
lariam (anti-malaria)
levodopa (Dopar, Sinemet, Atamet)
lidocaine (Xylocaine)
mefloquine (Lariam)
meperidine (Demerol)
meprobamate (Miltown)
methyldopa (Aldomet)
metoclopramide (Reglan)
metoprolol (Lopressor)
metrizamide (Amipaque)
metronidazole (Flagyl)
narcotics
neuroleptics
nonsteroid anti-inflammatory agents
opiates
pentazocine (Talwin)
Pergolide (Permax)
Phenthiazines (not all linked to depression)
Phenylpropanolamine (Dexatrim)
physostigmine
Prazosin
progestins, implanted (Norplant)
Propoxyphene (Darvon)
propranolol (Inderal)
quanethidine
ranitidine
reserpine (Diupres, Hydropres)
steroids (prednisone)
succinimide derivatives
sulfonamides
Tagamet
theophylline (Theophyl)
thiazide diuretics
thiothixene (Navane)
triazolam (Halcion)

Based on a careful medical evaluation, often including a complete medical history and physical examination, the following definitions would be used to diagnose a minor depression, dysthymic disorder, or major depression.

Diagnosing Mild, Chronic Depression or Dysthymia

Dysthymia is being depressed most days, for most of the day, *for at least two years* and not without symptoms for more than two months at a time. In children and adolescents, dysthymia may be characterized by irritability (instead of sadness) and has to persist only for at least *one year*. You would have at least two of the symptoms listed in the previous chapter on p. 19.

The *Diagnostic and Statistical Manual of Mental Disorders, Fourth Edition (DSM-IV)* also notes these specifics about the diagnosis of dysthymia:

- During the past two years (one year for children and teenagers), you did not have a major depressive episode so the symptoms aren't better explained as being a partial remission from a previous major depression.
- If you developed dysthymia first (for at least two years, one year in children or adolescents) and then had a major depressive episode, you may be diagnosed with both major depression and dysthymia (double depression).
- You never had a manic or hypomanic (a milder form of mania) episode (as diagnosed by a professional).
- Your dysthymic symptoms are not because of another mental illness such as schizophrenia or delusional disorder.
- Your dysthymic symptoms are not the result of a medical condition, medication, or the result of any substance abuse.

Many of the conditions mentioned above are very serious illnesses and should be treated by a trained professional as soon as possible.

EARLY ONSET DYSTHYMIA

When dysthymia develops before the age of 21, it's called early onset dysthymia. To understand the underlying causes of dysthymia, a distinction is made between early onset dysthymia and late onset dysthymia. Although both types exhibit similar severity and impairment, the early onset form can be harder to treat and is often complicated by longer episodes of major depression, substance abuse problems, family history of mood disorders, and higher rates of other psychological problems.

Most cases of dysthymia in adults, in fact, do stem from early onset dysthymia, meaning that you first experienced dysthymia before age 21 years (sometimes it occurs as early as age 5!). Early onset dysthymia develops very gradually and often eventually leads to major depression, if left untreated. People with early onset dysthymia tend to come from families with a history of mood disorders and were neglected or abused as children; some experienced trauma and were never treated.

LATE ONSET DYSTHYMIA

If you first developed dysthymia in adult life, at age 21 or later, your dysthymia would be considered late onset. This form can be much easier to turn around because the thought and behavior patterns characteristic of dysthymia haven't been entrenched in your life for decades. Rather, the changed state of mind is relatively new.

"If we think of major depression as a spectacular brain crash, milder depression can be compared to a form of mind-wearing water torture. Day in and day out it grinds us down, robbing us of our will to succeed in life, to interact with others, and to enjoy the things that others take for granted. The gloom that is generated in our tortured brains spills outward into the space that surrounds us and warns away all those who might otherwise be our friends and associates and loved ones. All too frequently we find ourselves alone, shunned by the world around us and lacking the strength to make our presence felt . . .

"Still, we are able to function, a sort of death-in-life existence that gets us out into the world and to work and the duties of staying alive then back to our homes and the blessed relief of flopping into our unmade beds.

"All too often, we are told to snap out of it. That the invisible water torture we carry in our heads is our own fault. And shamed into thinking something is wrong with our attitudes, we fail to seek help. Or, if we do, it's our family physician who confuses a very real chemical imbalance in the brain with some imaginary defect in our personality . . .

"And, sooner or later, it happens, the brain crash. Major depression. That's how most of us wind up, according to the experts, sometimes with a double depression, a depression on top of a depression that never had to be. One that could have been stopped years before.

"And that, perhaps, is the saddest news of all: None of this ever had to happen."

—John McManamy, reprinted with permission, http://www.suite101.com/article.cfm/depression/17588

PERSONALITY DISORDER AND DYSTHYMIA

The *DSM-IV* has no diagnosis for a depressive personality disorder, but its index has a notation that this is an area in need of more research. Some mental health professionals advocate including depressive personality disorder in the next edition and defining it as having a constant pattern of depressive thoughts and behaviors, while the definition of dysthymia would emphasize having some of the physical symptoms of depression, such as sleep and eating problems and low energy. For the time being, though, this distinction isn't made and the more inclusive definition of dysthymia is used.

Other mental health professionals do not advocate making this distinction. They assert that many people who are treated appropriately with psychotherapy *do* change: they aren't glum or pessimistic, and they cease having self-defeating thoughts and behaviors. This implies that, indeed, dysthymia is not a personality trait but rather a very treatable long-term problem.

CHRONIC FATIGUE SYNDROME AND DYSTHYMIA

When Chronic Fatigue Syndrome (CFS) was first recognized in the 1980s, it was hard to distinguish it from dysthymia because of months of extreme fatigue, depression, aches and pain, and sometimes a low-grade fever and other symptoms. Also, chronic fatigue syndrome can easily trigger depression because of the helplessness in not knowing what is wrong and because of the difficulty of living with a chronic illness.

However, with a better understanding of CFS, the Centers for Disease Control (CDC) distinguish the disorder by its flulike symptoms, such as headache, fever or feverishness, sore throat, muscle aches, joint pains, muscle weakness, swollen lymph nodes, and sore throat. The CDC also notes, however, that depression (and anxiety, among other psychiatric disorders) may predispose one to CFS.

Diagnosing Minor Depression

A minor depression is essentially a shorter-lived version of being depressed most of the time for at least two weeks or reaping little or no pleasure or interest in things *and* having at least one to five depressive symptoms listed in the previous chapter (and below under major depression). The symptoms have to be severe enough to cause significant distress.

Diagnosing Severe Depression or Major Depressive Disorder

If you suspect you have a major depression, see a physician or trained mental health professional immediately.

At the risk of being repetitive, we repeat the criteria for major depression.

Major Depression
Having at least five of these symptoms for at least two weeks.
Either #1 or #2 has to be present:

1. **Depressed mood most of the day on most days. (In children and adolescents, this may be irritability instead.)**

2. **Rarely feel pleasure or joy.**

3. Significant weight gain or loss of appetite (5% change in body weight in one month).

4. Either can't sleep or sleep too much, on most days.

5. Noticeably agitated or passive and slowed down on most days.

6. Almost always feels tired and low energy.

7. Feel guilt or worthlessness nearly all the time.

8. Difficulty concentrating almost all the time.

9. Thinks frequently about death and/or suicide.

The *DSM-IV* also notes these specifics about diagnosing major depression: the symptoms
- Don't follow a manic episode
- Cause significant distress or problems at work, at home, or in social relationships
- Are not caused by drugs, alcohol, medications, or medical conditions
- Are not occurring within two months of grieving a loved one

When major depressions last longer than two years, they are considered chronic depressions. Usually, these cases are double depressions: dysthymia with intermittent episodes of major depression.

Next, we'll look at the causes of dysthymia and the various factors that put you at higher risk.

4

◆ ◆ ◆

Who Gets Dysthymia and Why:
Causes and Risk Factors

Men ought to know
That from nothing else
But the brain
Come joys,
Delights,
Laughter and sports,
Grief,
Despondency
And lamentation

—Hippocrates, *On the Sacred Disease*

What exactly causes dysthymia? What makes one person resilient and another vulnerable? Although you can't do anything about some of the causes and risk factors, you certainly can do a lot about others, particularly monitoring self-talk and "automatic" thoughts that put you in bad and discouraging moods (chapter 5). But that's getting ahead of ourselves. First, we'll explore specific causes of dysthymia and factors that make you especially vulnerable.

Causes of Dysthymia

There is no simple, single reason why some people develop persistent depression and others don't. Dysthymia is caused by a variety of genetic, biological, psychosocial, and circumstantial factors. Although each person's profile of risk factors is unique, dysthymia can be thought of as a biopsychosocial disorder, like other forms of depression.

First of all, *dysthymia is not your fault*. Feeling glum or sluggish most of the time isn't because of some mental laziness or lack of character: dysthymia simply isn't a component of your personality. (In 1980, experts redefined it from a personality trait to a mood disorder.) Most researchers believe that your genetic makeup may make you vulnerable or predisposed to dysthymia but that external stressors trigger and maintain the disorder. By the same token, certain factors can protect you from becoming chronically depressed, such as your style of explanatory thinking and your social support system.

Causes of Dysthymia		
Physical Genetic/ Biochemical	**Psychological**	**Life Circumstances**
Brain physiology	Pessimism	Abuse
Genetic inheritance	Global thinking style	Trauma
Medical illnesses	Neuroticism	Severe Loss
Medications	Dysfunctional attitudes	Neglect
		Stigma

PHYSICAL CAUSES

Biochemical changes.   Every thought, emotion, and behavior affects the brain's biochemistry, which in turn can influence your thoughts, feelings, and behaviors. Just as normal emotions such as love, fear, and rage flood your body with biochemical signals, so too can depressive feelings and self-hatred. In fact, stressors such as pain, social isolation, and grief not only influence the brain's biochemistry but even can change its hard wiring. These changes can make the brain more sensitive to subsequent stress and predispose the person to respond poorly to stress the next time. Over time, these changes can actually cause alterations in the structure of the brain.

Driving these changes in the brain are biochemical substances, mostly hormones (particularly the stress-response hormone cortisol) and chemical messengers called neurotransmitters, such as serotonin, acetylcholine, and norepinephrine. Neurotransmitters bridge the gap between nerve cells (or neurons), which permits the electrochemical impulses of neural systems to function. Impairments and imbalances in some of these neurotransmitters, such as serotonin, are strongly linked to both chronic stress and depression. Most of the medications used to treat depression have dramatic and rapid effects on the activity of neurons by influencing serotonin or norepinephrine, or both.

Also linked to depression are increased levels of certain hormones that stress triggers, such as cortisol, and lower levels of other hormones, such as thyroid hormone. Before menopause, many women experience a regular monthly mood pattern that is linked to rising and falling levels of estrogen. As estrogen may enhance serotonin function in the brain, the normal decline in hormone levels before a monthly period may provoke a state of relative serotonin deficit. In fact, that may be one reason why women have triple the rate of dysthymia than men. (See chapter 12.)

Physiological activity of the brain.   Cutting-edge research also suggests that moods and thoughts are influenced not only by neurotransmitters and hormones but also by the cellular activity of various parts of the brain. The activity of particular areas of the brain can now be studied by measuring the rate of blood flow or energy metabolism; modern techniques permit areas as small as the nail on your little finger to be visualized. Depressed persons often have decreased blood flow to several areas in their brain, especially the frontal regions. Brain activity appears to be shifted to other areas of the brain involved in processing emotional arousal. These changes may also be accompanied by a relative increase in the activity of the nondominant side of the brain (usually the right). Taken together, these changes in brain activity might explain why some depressed people seem to be virtually unable to use good advice or standard problem-solving strategies to reduce their difficulties. It is as if an arousal circuit of the brain is stuck in the on position and deactivates other, more complex circuits. (See chapter 9.)

Genetic inheritance.   Along with a family's genetic heritage for hair and eye color are predispositions to anxiety and mood disorders. Dysthymia is much more common in families with dysthymia or major depression. Most researchers do not believe that the illness is inherited per se, but rather it is a predisposition. Further, these higher risks may not only be due to specific genes but also because of the family environment and shared histories. Much research still has to be done.

Twin studies

Studies of twins show the genetic link to depression. Identical twins, which derive from one fertilized egg, have the exact same genetic code. Fraternal twins, which originate from two fertilized eggs, are not much more alike than any other pair of siblings, except they have shared the same environment during upbringing (especially same-sex fraternal twin pairs). Nature's best genetic experiment thus compares identical twins, fraternal twins, and same-sex siblings to disentangle the effects of genes and environment.

When one identical twin has depression, the other has a 70 percent chance of also suffering from a similar condition. When a sibling or fraternal twin suffers from depression, the other has only a 25 percent chance of developing the disorder.

Medical illnesses and medications.   Medications can also influence biology and biochemistry in ways that cause or mimic dysthymia and depression, as we examined in the previous chapter. In addition, having a medical illness can be stressful, which may also make you more vulnerable to dysthymia or depression. A person who has had a heart attack, for example, has about a 40 percent chance of developing depression. More chronic medical illnesses, such as arthritis or diabetes, are overrepresented among those with chronic depressions.

PSYCHOSOCIAL CAUSES

Your family relationships, your personal coping style (how you explain events in your life to yourself), and your problem-solving responses can be major players in dysthymia. Although how much the psychosocial changes trigger biochemical changes and vice versa can't yet be distinguished, one pathway obviously influences another. Monkey studies show, for example, that those with high brain levels of serotonin are consistently more socially dominant; likewise, a fall from a dominant rank lowers the animal's levels of serotonin.

History of depression.   If you have ever experienced an episode of depression, you are at about two to four times greater risk of developing depression again. And each time a person becomes clinically depressed, there is up to 15 percent chance that the depression will become chronic. Some research suggests that the brain increasingly acclimates to depression with each episode, so each episode increases the likelihood of another.

Poor coping strategies and cognitive distortions.   Loss is part of the human condition and at the core of most first episodes of depression. Often a key life event has caused humiliation or a dramatic loss of self-esteem. If you have a pessimistic way of explaining events to yourself, such as blaming yourself for your disappointments and losses, you can be setting yourself up for more problems. In coping with a major setback, you may increase the risk of depression by telling yourself that the loss is irreplaceable and will change your life (for the worse) forever. People who tend to ruminate about the loss (i.e., to replay the event over and over again) also are at greater risk of depression, perhaps by continuously rekindling the pain and humiliation. By beating yourself up for what you did or didn't do, you turn setbacks into catastrophes that make you feel smaller and more sick at heart.

People who usually don't get depressed by such losses tend to put the events in a less threatening perspective, catching themselves if they generalize negativity into all aspects of their lives. They view the event or loss as over and done with and see it for what it was: a one-time event that doesn't poison their thinking but from which they can learn and move on. That explanatory style of thinking protects them from depression. An active coping style that centers on problem solving and involvement in distracting activities also tends to lower the risk of depression. (See chapter 5.)

Anxiety.   Anxiety and depression often go hand in hand. This is because fear and sadness are closely related emotions: one helps you respond to threat, the other guides your response to loss. One study found, for example, that more than 95 percent of depressed patients also suffer from anxiety. And vice versa, more than one-half of those with anxiety disorders experience major bouts of depression.

CIRCUMSTANTIAL CAUSES

As we said earlier, a tragedy or loss, most often in childhood or adolescence, frequently sets the course to dysthymia. The seed may lie dormant forever, or it may become a threat if chronic stress wears you down, perhaps altering your brain's biochemistry, or a genetic predisposition has made you vulnerable in the first place. Most likely you were just a child or teenager at the time of the tragedy or loss and not adequately protected by a support network of strong positive relationships. The aftermath of the tragedy may have smothered your good spirits, which never recovered. Typical life tragedies at the core of dysthymia are

- A severe loss, such the death of a parent or sibling in childhood, the loss of a child, mate, or close friend in adulthood
- Physical, sexual, or emotional abuse or neglect as a child
- A major trauma such as surviving war, a violent crime, an airplane crash, a sniper, or act of terrorism (dysthymia is a common residual effect of post-traumatic stress disorder; see section on 9/11 on pp. 49–52)

Karen, 36, remembers that back in adolescence, she felt misunderstood and emotionally distant from her high-achieving parents. And she always wondered if her worries about the inappropriate sexual contact she had with her uncle when she was between ages 10 and 14 had something to do with her first episode of major depression, which began at age 15. She never really bounced back.

How High Is Your Risk?

So with all these causes of dysthymia, why doesn't everyone have it? In fact, most people don't have dysthymia, even though they have suffered the same life tragedies that are inherent to the human condition. The answer is because some people have multiple risk factors, which makes them highly susceptible. Others have a positive take on life, which makes them more resilient. (See chapter 5.)

THE RISKS IN CHILDHOOD

Three out of four adults with dysthymia first developed it before age 21. There are several risk factors for early onset dysthymia.

Early chronic stress or trauma.   If you witnessed violence, lost a parent, or were sexually or physically abused, or endured other traumas, you'd be at particularly high risk. Rejection, stigma, and neglect could also have devastated your tender self-esteem. Children can be very vulnerable, and without enough nurturing support around them, some kids will never overcome certain experiences.

An incomplete recovery from an early episode of major depression.   Many adults with dysthymia can recall a defining time when they first felt depressed, either mildly or severely. If it was mild, it started a long chain of increasingly serious mood problems. If it was severe, they may never have recovered but were left with a lingering apathy, passivity, irritability (especially in young people), and impaired ability to cope with life's endless tasks—with a lingering dysthymia.

Moodiness and depressive feelings as a teenager.   Other people with dysthymia look back and remember being a moody teenager and then never really changing.

Family history.   Depressions often run in families. This could be because of common genetics, the shared stressful living environment, or having similar dysfunctional coping or cognitive strategies. It is possible that some of us inherit a lower set point for day-to-day moods, what some researchers used to refer to as a depressive personality temperament.

Attention deficit hyperactivity disorder (ADHD).   Studies show that boys with ADHD are three times more likely to develop depression, including dysthymia, than other children. Although there may be some inherited common risk factor, it is also true that many who suffer from ADHD develop low self-esteem and a sense of being unable to succeed in academic pursuits.

THE RISKS IN ADULTHOOD

One of four adults with dysthymia developed it for the first time after age 21. The most common risk factors for late onset dysthymia are:

Acute stress.   Typically caused by a single event, such as surviving or witnessing violence (war, plane crash, snipers, accidents, natural disasters, or devastating terrorist attacks), or personal tragedy, such as loss of a family member, acute stress can contribute to late onset dysthymia.

Chronic stress.   Caring for years for a disabled relative, grieving for several members of your immediate family, or living with persistent and severe financial problems, a chronic disease, stigma of some sort, marital problems, sexual or physical abuse, unemployment or overwork produce chronic stress and can contribute to late onset dysthymia.

> Peggy, a 44-year-old teacher, believes her unhappiness started when her husband began traveling constantly or working late, leaving her home alone with their two young children. Everything became drudgery, and she no longer reaped much pleasure from what used to bring her joy. But she never really noticed the gray shadow of pessimism darkening her world. It just seemed she always felt this way.

How does stress cause dysthymia? Studies show that stress triggers structural and biochemical changes in the brain, which becomes increasingly harder to normalize. Whereas researchers find a strong link between a major life stressor and a first episode of depression, they can't find such a link between later stressful events and a fourth or fifth episode of depression. That's because each episode of stress takes a toll on the brain, which doesn't recover fully; thus each episode takes the brain farther from normal, making it more prone to depression.

Family history of depression and other mood disorders.   Your risk of dysthymia is up to seven times higher if you have family members with dysthymia, and three to five times higher if you have family members with depression, than someone with no family history of depression.

History of depression.   As explained above, research suggests that each episode of depression increasingly predisposes the brain to experience depression again.

Substance abuse.   At least one-third of those with dysthymia have a history of substance abuse (alcohol, recreational drugs, tranquilizers, and other psychoactive drug abuse). Whether substance abuse contributed to or was a result of dysthymia is not always so clear-cut. Dysthymia may prompt some people to turn to drugs or alcohol to get high after feeling numb for so long or to hush the nagging inner voice.

Poverty.   It's hard to live without enough money for safe housing, good schools, and adequate medical care. Low income means drudgery jobs, poorer health, stress, financial insecurity, and feelings of helplessness and even hopelessness. People living in poverty also are more likely to be victimized by crime or physical violence than those who are financially better off. Researchers find depression is more common in low-income ethnic or cultural groups, probably because they feel as if they have less control over their lives and events around them. Research suggests that while poverty and unemployment don't play a role in causing depression, they both contribute to how long an existing depression lasts.

Being female.   Women are three times more likely to develop dysthymia in adulthood than men. Contributing causes may be that men tend to be more self-reliant, less introspective, and more action-oriented when upset; women tend to be passive and dependent, to mull over problems repeatedly (rumination), to have lower paying jobs with more role conflicts, feelings of inadequacy, and lack of control in their work. Stress over dieting and self-image may contribute to greater feelings of inadequacy and lack of control, some experts suggest. Female hormones probably also play a role; researchers note that the risk of dysthymia in childhood (before puberty) and in later adult life (after menopause) are comparable among men and women. (See chapter 12.)

Lack of social support.   Studies consistently show that good social support protects against social isolation and depression, while poor social support is a risk factor.

Medication.   As detailed in the previous chapter, many medications can cause depressive symptoms and put you at higher risk.

What puts you at higher risk for dysthymia?

For children and teens	For adults
Early chronic stress or trauma	Acute stress
An early mild depression	Chronic stress
Moodiness or depressive feelings as a teenager	Substance abuse
An early major depression	History of depression
Family history	Family history
Attention deficit hyperactivity disorder (ADHD)	Low income
	Being female
Possible risk factors	
Headaches	Headaches
Sleep problems	Sleep problems
Dieting	Dieting
Traumatic events or disasters	Traumatic events or disasters

OTHER POSSIBLE RISK FACTORS

Headaches.   People with tension or migraine headaches are much more likely to also be depressed than those without such headaches. However, no one knows if depression causes the headaches or the headaches cause the depression. Some experts suggest that both are caused by common factors, perhaps even the same genetic defect.

Sleep problems.   Sleep disorders and depression also seem to go hand in hand, and again, we don't know if that's because they both stem from the same genetic defect or one causes the other. Yet, more than 90 percent of people suffering from depression also suffer from insomnia.

Dieting.   As we discuss in more detail in chapter 12, dieting is a risk factor for women because if you deprive yourself, you may get moody or irritable; if you binge, you feel guilty and ashamed. If you berate yourself for being overweight or having no will power, you are putting yourself down and making yourself feel inadequate, out of control, of low worth, insecure, and a failure. All these factor are risks for dysthymia.

Modern Life and the Fallout from September 11, 2001

Modern life is stressful, with families scattered all over the country; divorce rates of over 50 percent; two-career families trying to do it all; threats of pollution and global warming; traffic jams, long lines, and popular media dominating culture and interfering with interpersonal contact. Add to all those stressors news that can generate intense fears about terrorist attacks, plane crashes, weapons of mass destruction, anthrax, shoe bombers, devastating viruses, etc.

Unfortunately, the events of September 11, 2001, will trigger untold cases of dysthymia and depression in the years to come. One-third to one-half of the survivors, rescue workers, bereaved ones, and those who witnessed the horrors of that day suffered from post-traumatic stress disorder (see below). And as we'll see, dysthymia is a common long-term effect of PTSD.

More than any event in contemporary history of the United States, 9/11 puts the entire nation at higher risk for dysthymia, anxiety, depression, and substance abuse. Not only was the event the most devastating single attack we ever experienced, but our daily lives (and our perceptions of our lives, in many cases) have changed. And, for the

What is post-traumatic stress disorder (PTSD)?

PTSD can occur after one has been through a terrifying, life-threatening experience that threatened or caused severe physical harm and, at least a month later, has persistent and severe problems at home or work or in another area of daily living.

Flashbacks, nightmares, guilt, and depression trouble many who have experienced trauma. Substance abuse, divorce, and suicide are more common in those with PTSD. Some signs of PTSD include:

- The shakes or heart palpitations when reminded of the event
- Flashbacks or nightmares or other sleep problems
- Feeling emotionally numb
- Feeling overwhelmed in normal situations
- Crying uncontrollably
- Feeling isolated from family and friends
- Trying to avoid any reminders of the event
- Not being able to remember important details about the event
- Feeling pessimistic that typical life goals, such as marriage, children, and aging, will not be reached
- Being startled easily
- Being irritable or expressing sudden outbursts of anger
- Having trouble concentrating
- Hypervigilance
- Feeling extremely moody, irritable, angry, suspicious, or frightened
- Survivor guilt
- Fearfulness or hopelessness about the future

Rates of depression and dysthymia are disproportionately high among people who have had PTSD

first time in our history, we all witnessed the trauma—some of us in real time—and then watched the horrors over and over again as we tried to grapple with what happened.

Dr. David Satcher, the surgeon general of the United States at the time, warned mental health professionals that the aftereffects of the attacks would reverberate for many months to come. That's because we feel more fragile, scared, unsafe, and insecure than ever before. We feel helpless and less hopeful about the future as new threats, fear, and anxiety pervade our daily lives.

Even though most of us weren't threatened directly on 9/11, we mourn the loss of life, we feel more sharply the raw pain of each be-

---

What signs of dysthymia will stem from the terrorist attacks?

Mental health professionals predict that the terrorist attacks will result in more

- Substance abuse
- Insomnia
- Family violence
- Problem behaviors that will result in people losing their jobs
- Abnormal behaviors
- Dysthymia and major depression

---

reaved family on TV, and we cried with them. We didn't know the victims or their families, but we feel stressed and vulnerable. Those feelings are exacerbated each morning as we're assaulted by the bad news of poverty, crime, unemployment, a sagging economy, deaths in our families, seriously ill children, accidents, and so on. We are also haunted by the horrors and losses of that day; these feelings make our own personal losses and horrors ache even more.

The new age of terrorism

Terrorism puts us all at higher risk for dysthymia because it

- Destroys our sense of security, trust, freedom, and well-being
- Wreaks havoc on the comfort we derive from living in a predictable and controllable world
- Enrages us when we think of the injustice and agony the terrorism causes innocent victims
- Triggers a range of negative emotions, such as anxiety, anger, vulnerability, frustration, restlessness, hopelessness, helplessness, and pervasive fears, which take a powerful physiological toll.

Indeed, the effects of the deliberate violence are more damaging to mental health than violence caused by natural events. And people have developed new fears of flying, traveling, opening mail, going into tall buildings.

Guilt is also a common residual from 9/11 and linked to dysthymia. We live not only with survivor guilt but with guilt that we may not be feeling the pain of the traumatic losses deeply enough. The guilt makes us question our self-worth—we're "bad" because we're not sensitive or patriotic enough. That's an additional psychological burden warn the experts.

The acute anxiety has waned over these many months, but the toxic fallout for many of us is a deep sense of sadness and a profound loss of control and hope. We have become ever more negative and less hopeful than we were a few years ago.

Mental health professionals are particularly concerned about 9/11 because what they have learned from the survivors of the Oklahoma City bombing is foreboding. Five years after the Oklahoma City federal building was bombed, although the attacker was American and the event didn't conjure up fears of ubiquitous foreign terrorists, and despite a wealth of mental health support in Oklahoma, the people of Oklahoma City are not doing particularly well. Almost 30 percent developed PTSD and 50 percent developed depression or alcoholism. Two years later, according to one study, more than 15 percent of the children and teenagers living within 100 miles of Oklahoma City were suffering from significant PTSD symptoms related to the bombing, although most of these children had no direct contact with the bombing, its victims, or survivors. Oklahoma City officials report that they still receive thousands of calls each year to help cope with the 1995 events. The aftereffects from 9/11 are likely to be thicker as the amorphous but looming threat of possible additional attacks, the images of the deaths, misery, helplessness, and hopelessness we saw on TV hover and continue to darken our lives.

Who is at highest risk?

- Those who were close to the events
- Those who had loved ones close to the event
- Those who are emotionally fragile, cry frequently, obsess over sirens, new attacks, or terrorist rumors, have depressive symptoms a year later
- Those who were troubled by preexisting stressors, such as a death in the family, chronic illness, a troublesome relationship, a difficult childhood (parental separation, physical or sexual abuse, neglect or major illness)
- Women who are already at higher risk for dysthymia and who tend to be more empathetic

The more risk factors you have, the more fragile your sense of well-being is and the more vulnerable you are to feelings of helplessness and powerlessness. If you see personal and world problems as permanent and pervasive, you are at grave risk. This learned helplessness—the belief that nothing you can do can make a difference—is at the root of much of today's dysthymia.

Next, we'll look at treatments for dysthymia, starting with what you can do to help yourself and where you can seek relief.

PART TWO

◆ ◆ ◆

How to Feel Better

5

◆ ◆ ◆

The Psychology of Feeling Good

Men are disturbed not by things, but by the
view which they take of them.

—Epictetus, *The Enchiridion*

The mind is its own place,
And in itself can make
A Heav'n of Hell,
Or a Hell of Heav'n.

—John Milton, *Paradise Lost*

Life is a matter of attention.

—ToDo Institute*

This chapter focuses on the strategies that have proven successful in relieving dysthymia and depression. These strategies could, in fact, help anyone cope better with life's hardships. They are derived from the psychotherapies—cognitive-behavioral, interpersonal, and problem-solving therapies—that have shown success in a multitude of studies in turning around the downward, self-perpetuating, and destructive spiral of dysthymia and depression.

If your depression is mild, you can probably help yourself immediately by using these strategies and skills that will focus on three areas:

- *Feelings and Thoughts:* Distorted Thoughts and Where They Lead

- *Behavior:* Do What Would Help You to Feel Better

- *Relationships:* When Troubled Relationships Darken Your World

---

*A nonprofit educational organization that provides a wide range of educational programs and services related to Constructive Living, Morita therapy, Naikan, Meaningful Life therapy, and other related areas. See Appendix 3.

Distorted Thoughts and
Where They Lead

Ask yourself: Can you have an emotion without a prior belief or thought? Where do your emotions really come from? They don't come from your heart; we all know the heart is just a muscular blood pump (if you had a heart transplant, you wouldn't have your donor's emotions). Rather, your feelings come from your thoughts in your mind and brain.

You think about how you lost that promotion or you were jilted and you get angry, feel humiliated and ashamed, or wronged. And you feel worse.

You fret that your problems have no end in sight. You will never get another job. You will never lose any weight. You will always be alone. You will never make enough money. These kinds of beliefs feel 100 percent true—and that leads to more thoughts that are less and less hopeful, more pessimistic, discouraging, and helpless. And you feel almost automatically worse.

You recycle thoughts about how other people are smarter or prettier, or richer or thinner, and you almost instantaneously feel inadequate and less worthy. And you feel even more depressed.

But just because you think something doesn't mean that it's accurate or right, even if it feels like the truth. It is just a thought.

> How you think about things can literally make you happy or miserable; studies show that this single factor is one of *the most significant* components of mental health.

The good news is that studies prove you can learn to change your style of thinking by following simple rules to ensure that you don't distort your thoughts and make yourself miserable. It may sound like New Age psychobabble to some people, but it is now common practice in psychotherapy used for dysthymia, depression, and anxiety disorders to identify self-defeating styles of thinking and to learn how to change them. If you wait to feel better, you frequently end up just waiting. It is, however, much easier to do nothing and wallow in your automatic responses of anxiety, fear, or shame, which flood your system with harmful stress (fight or flight) hormones. The harder but by far healthier and happier route is to use your will and your mind by applying reason and self-observation.

There is a much better way: think for change. This approach not only works but also may be more durable—and faster—than the effects of medication.

IS THERE ANOTHER WAY TO SEE THINGS?

When something bad happens and you feel terrible or ashamed or sad, your feelings stem from what you think about. And often these thoughts are automatic. Just as we have habits of behavior, we also have habits of thinking. We're often so unaware of our automatic thoughts (such as I'm fat or stupid or wronged or ugly or a lousy friend or athlete), we come to think, "That's how it is." Period. No grounds for debate.

But if you are feeling bad, sad, mad, guilty, hurt, agitated, anxious, frustrated, apathetic, passive, negative, it's almost certain that you are thinking negatively. Stop and ask yourself: What was I thinking before my mood dropped? Does the thought explain my mood? Is there another way to think about it?

If you say, "No! That's the way I feel. Nothing can change it. It's hopeless. I'm helpless," then take another look—because there is evidence that sadness, anxiety, and pessimism alter the way we think, completing the self-perpetuating cycle.

The event itself, however, is usually not so terrible that it would make other people feel bad, sad, mad, etc. Your style of interpreting the event is what made you feel helpless, lonely, guilty, or ashamed. You may not be a victim of a callous, uncaring world but of your negative thoughts. How you perceive the world is shaped by your own thinking patterns, which could be distorted and inaccurate. If so, you can focus on changing these negative thoughts.

Life doesn't invariably make you happy or sad. It's what you tell yourself and consequently what you do about it that creates an emotional and behavioral response. Think about it—not everyone becomes depressed during a divorce, a bankruptcy, or following a layoff. For most, even the grief over a dead parent, spouse, or child does not lead to a full-fledged clinical depression. Sadness is *not* depression. And people do not inherit depression—they inherit the vulnerability or predisposition to become depressed. One's thoughts about oneself, one's environment, relationships, or the future either diminish or intensify that vulnerability.

So ask again, "What am I telling myself and is there another way to look at this?" If you say no again, then find some proof (other than your own thoughts) that there's no other way. Is your answer simply another automatic, negative thought, or is it a careful assessment of

the evidence? Are you merely responding emotionally and automatically, or carefully and consciously? The automatic thoughts are frequently
the distortions we tell ourselves. They're just thoughts that occurred to
you ("I could never do that." "She's always so pretty and well dressed;
I feel crummy." "Why does this always happen to me?") and our
thoughts seem true.

At the expense of being redundant, we show again the downward
spiral of negative thinking:

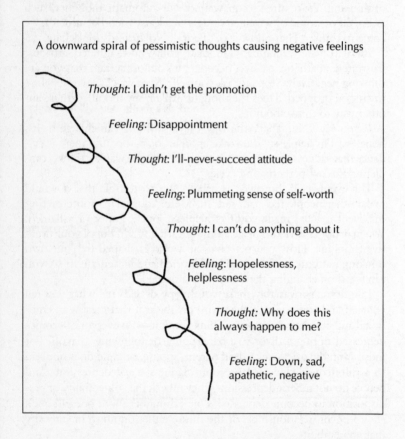

A downward spiral of pessimistic thoughts causing negative feelings

Thought: I didn't get the promotion

Feeling: Disappointment

Thought: I'll-never-succeed attitude

Feeling: Plummeting sense of self-worth

Thought: I can't do anything about it

Feeling: Hopelessness, helplessness

Thought: Why does this always happen to me?

Feeling: Down, sad, apathetic, negative

But you don't have to believe the first thought that comes to mind
and allow your thoughts to drift downward, taking your mood with
them. Distorted thoughts can be tested for accuracy and can be chal-
lenged and revised—with reliable mood lifting effects.

"True realism consists in revealing the surprising things which habit keeps covered and prevents us from seeing."

—Jean Cocteau, French author, filmmaker

You don't always have control over your feelings and you can't control what other people do, so don't try to change either one. In fact, negative feelings are often quite appropriate responses to insult, adversity, and heartbreak. However unpleasant or sad, though, you don't have to behave based on emotions alone. Emotions are just one part of the larger picture and you can't just change them by will. Emotions are for feeling. You feel what you feel; feelings don't need to be fixed.

Rather, focus on the other part of the picture—how you talk to yourself—because you *can* change that. When you correct distorted thinking, feelings and behavior will change and, as a result, you will feel better.

When you feel angry, worthless, helpless, ashamed, ask yourself, "Are my thoughts about this valid? Am I exaggerating, seeing it in the worst possible way, seeing it as black and white, jumping to conclusions, or seeing the problem truly accurately? What can I do to solve this problem, whether I feel like it or not? What does the reality call for?"

This is not "the power of positive thinking," and we are not suggesting that you practice self-deception or Pollyanna-ism. Rather, we simply suggest that you practice realistic, nondefeatist constructive thinking. The goal is to catch negative thoughts and then challenge yourself; check the proof (or, more likely, the lack of proof!) to determine whether you are exaggerating or distorting something. Then try to reframe your thoughts in a more realistic and nondistorted way.

"Your way of explaining events to yourself determines how helpless you can become, or how energized, when you encounter the everyday setbacks as well as momentous defeats."

—Martin Seligman, *Learned Optimism*

YOU FEEL WHAT YOU THINK

If you think pessimistically, you are at high risk for dysthymia and depression, studies at the University of Pennsylvania and elsewhere have repeatedly proven. If you don't think negatively, you are more likely to be resilient in the face of setbacks and disappointments. Constructive thinking patterns can actually serve as a sort of psychological inoculation against pessimism and depression.

If you lose your job, your championship, or your mate, for example, and you think . . .

"If I wasn't so stupid and careless, this wouldn't have happened"
"That ruins everything"
"I'm a loser"
"I'm a failure; it's all my fault"
"School is useless"
"People are out to cheat and beat me and put me down"
"Nothing goes my way"

you are promoting depression by interpreting the event as a *permanent, pervasive, and personal* failure, writes Martin Seligman, professor of psychology at the University of Pennsylvania. You become pessimistic and prone to depression when you typically view setbacks as someone's fault (usually your own) and due to something that you can't change, which makes you feel helpless and hopeless. Many people generalize their reaction from *one event* to affect all aspects of their lives, perhaps without an end in sight. In other words, you may generalize your negativity to a permanent and pervasive condition. These are hallmarks of the thinking style that accompany a depressive response.

If you predict that "it's going to be terrible" or "it'll never work out," it's as if you're invested in proving yourself right that you'll be miserable. It's not that you want to fail, but people do strive to be consistent with their beliefs. Part of this consistency is your mental set—you're more likely to remember past failures and see roadblocks that will interfere with successful coping. On the other hand, if you view a setback as due to something specific, leave it in the past, and consider what you can do now to produce a different outcome, you help immunize yourself against depression and create an optimistic view of life. Optimism creates the opportunity for behavioral changes.

A more optimistic view of setbacks that prompted the pessimistic comments above might be . . .

"If I wasn't so stupid and careless, this wouldn't have happened."
"It was just a fluke that this happened; I was overtired, stressed that night, and not paying attention." (It's more helpful to identify something specific as being the problem.)

"That ruins everything."
"It's too bad that happened, but it's not the end of the world. Next time, we'll try . . ."

"I'm a loser."
"I really messed that up. I'm not as good at this as she is."

"I'm a failure; it's all my fault."
"I got fired because I'm just not good at that type of thing."

"School is useless."
"This class/book/homework/teacher assignment is useless."

"People are out to cheat and beat me and put me down."
"She was really rude to me and cheated me."

"Nothing goes my way."
"This week has been really tough."

By learning to recognize faulty perceptions that can just as easily be developed into constructive thinking patterns, you can dramatically reduce your risk of dysthymia.

Stop yourself
when you view setbacks, disappointments, and failures as

personal
(about you or your fault)

permanent
(failing to realize that it won't always be this way)

pervasive
(allowing the negativity or the problem to
contaminate all aspects of your life)
That viewpoint makes you pessimistic and prone to dysthymia.

Remind yourself that
it's not always your fault, or due to a flaw in your personality,
or necessarily even about you.

Recognizing a style of explaining events to yourself—your style of self-talk—that promotes dysthymic and depressive responses is at the core of cognitive therapy, which has proven to help depression. Pessimistic self-talk is self-defeating; it also promotes bad moods, which increases the likelihood of self-defeating behaviors and the downward spinning spiral into dysthymia and depression.

> "Finding permanent and universal causes of good events along with temporary and specific causes for misfortune is the art of hope; finding permanent and universal causes for misfortune and temporary and specific causes of good events is the practice of despair."
>
> —Martin Seligman, *Authentic Happiness*

The technique is to

- *Recognize* that you're experiencing a disturbing emotion. Observe yourself having a feeling and then accept the feeling, but take charge of your response.

- *Notice* your thoughts. What triggered the emotion? Do a reality check: did you consider all the information available? are you ignoring, minimizing, or exaggerating something?

- *Identify* negative or distorted automatic thoughts. When the thoughts are observed, it is easier to recognize distortions.

- *Challenge* your negative thoughts. Where's the proof that this is true? Are my thoughts definitely accurate? How might my thoughts be mistaken? What are other possible explanations? This is not a process of rationalization but pausing to identify evidence that is realistic and valid and therefore might challenge your automatic, negative thoughts.

- *Reframe* your thought so it is not negative, personal, or pervasive. What would you tell a friend? We tend to be much more critical (unrealistically) with ourselves than our friends. Even if the disturbing thought is accurate, how likely is it that the worst will happen? What response does the situation call for? What interpretation really is in your best interest? What's the worst that could happen? If what you want doesn't occur, what opportunities or good things might come out of it?

Living on the positive side is healthier.

Not only does a positive frame of mind make you a happier person, but it also makes you a healthier person.

Optimists are more likely than pessimists to . . .
have lower blood pressure,
have uncompromised immune systems,
recover more quickly from surgery,
experience less pain,
need fewer medical and mental health services over the years,
live longer.

Remember: You are not a robot, doomed to respond automatically but are free to choose—and to change—your responses. By automatically responding to others, you give them the power to determine your happiness or well-being. Claim your freedom by using your own ability and power to choose how you view life's vicissitudes.

HOW TO THINK FOR CHANGE

Here are the most common cognitive distortions in the left-hand column; possibilities for reframing them are in the right-hand column.

Distorted Thinking Patterns	Constructive Thinking Patterns
All-or-Nothing, Black or White Thinking	**See the Gray and the Temporary**
You see the world as black or white.	This doesn't mean I'm a loser, unlovable.
You are a total failure, unlovable, thoughtless.	It's disappointing but I can work on . . .
You frequently think always, never, and forever.	I can start by . . .
I'll never succeed at this/be able to do this.	I can do better next time . . .
I don't have the talent.	Sometimes, I . . .
No negotiability in your framing.	Lately, I . . .
	Whatever caused the bad event, can be changed next time.
Ruminating: Recycling Disturbing Thoughts	**Challenge and Identify What's Worrying You**
You obsess over the same problem: something that already happened or something that might happen.	What's bothering me?
	Be a skeptic. Is it probable that the worst will happen?
	Is there really no alternative?

(continues)

Distorted Thinking Patterns	Constructive Thinking Patterns
By recycling negative thoughts, they become bigger and more persuasive in your mind. This makes it seem more and more true, when it's still just a figment of your mind.	What step could you take that would most benefit you?

Overgeneralizing

Because one bad thing happens, you believe everyone will always feel that way about you or it will always turn out that lousy way.

You think, Everybody knows . . .

You don't connect with anyone at a party and think, I'm a social outcast, bored and boring.

Your mate leaves a mess or forgets your birthday and you write him off as a total slob, inconsiderate, selfish.

Be Specific

One event doesn't mean from now on.

Give specific reasons, not a universal one, for what happened.

One person's criticism doesn't mean everyone.

What happened doesn't mean it will always happen as it did in that moment.

Stay in the present: don't assume always or never.

Mental Filtering/Tunnel Vision

A bad thing happens and as a result, you see the entire world through dark glasses. You only dwell on the bad, and become impervious to all the positive things that have happened and are happening.

Enlarge Your View

Don't stew over the bad thing and let it color your day. Keep a hassle in the parking lot in the lot. Don't take it to work or home. Pay attention to the good that happens, too.

Minimizing: Disqualifying the Positive

When something good happens, you explain it away or downplay your strengths and accomplishments. It was luck or a fluke.

It was no big deal.

They were just trying to be nice.

This leads to lower self-esteem and self-worth.

Enjoy the Glow, Believe the Positive

Enjoy the compliment. You worked hard and maybe you do deserve to appreciate your accomplishments. Give yourself credit. Say thank-you and mean it.

Distorted Thinking Patterns	Constructive Thinking Patterns
Jumping to Conclusions You assume the worst, most negative explanation for something. Someone's late—you assume they don't value you. Someone yawns while you're talking: you assume they're bored. Someone doesn't call: you believe they don't like you. You think, He/she hates me. He will never . . . , she looks down on me. You're convinced your interpretation is right. This leads to lower self-esteem, anger, resentment.	**Catch Yourself and Consider the Possibilities** Give others the benefit of the doubt. Don't make assumptions. How do you know that your interpretation is true rather than just your interpretation? If five people witness an accident, why do they have different versions?
Magnifying (Catastrophizing) You turn a setback or mistake into a catastrophe, a molehill into a mountain and then can't stop beating yourself up about it, turning a minor disappointment into a monster. This leads to anxiety and stress and catastrophic responses.	**Keep Life in Focus** War is horrible, death is serious. For most terrible things in life: so this too shall pass. Keep the disaster in today; don't let it leak into tomorrow and poison your future. You can't build a life on feeling good all the time. Don't turn sad into bad: the two are not the same.
Comparing Up I'll never be as successful . . . rich . . . thin . . . kind . . . as she is.	**Compare Down** I'm glad that I'm better off than . . . At least I can . . . What do I hold dear (rather than play catch up)?

(continues)

Distorted Thinking Patterns	Constructive Thinking Patterns

Mind Reading
You think you know what others are thinking:
    He thinks I'm . . .
    He resents that . . .
    People would think that I'm . . .
	You Can't Mind Read
	You can't possibly know what others think and feel so don't even try, because you might make up awful things about yourself—and believe them.

Fortunetelling What if . . . I will be overwhelmed and won't be able to . . . It wouldn't do any good. They couldn't help me. If I lose, he will fire me. I will do it wrong.	**Identify the Reality and Your Goal** I am well prepared. I will try to do my best. I hope today goes well. I'm good at this; even if I lose . . . No one has a crystal ball or a time machine. The present offers the best and only opportunity to respond.
Believing Feelings Are Reality You believe your emotions are the stark truth. If you feel guilty, you must have done something wrong. If you feel hurt, someone must have done something to you. You feel frustrated or overwhelmed by the job, and you assume resolving it is impossible. This leads to procrastination. And fear, too.	**Realize Feelings Aren't Facts** Using your feelings as a basis for your reasoning is faulty. Just because you feel something doesn't mean it's true. All it means is that you feel it. Now what are you going to do? Consider other possibilities. Break down overwhelming tasks.
Should Statements I should do this, I should do that will make you feel guilty and pressured and lead to shame and apathy. He should be more considerate. She should be more loving will lead to self-justified bitterness, anger, and resentment.	**Could Statements** I could do this, I could do that. As Michael Angier wrote: "Thou shalt not 'should' on thyself."*

*From Keys to Personal Effectiveness:
http://www.SuccessNet.org/keys.htm.

Distorted Thinking Patterns	Constructive Thinking Patterns
Labeling and Mislabeling	**A Behavior Is Bad, Not the Person**
You label yourself by your mistakes or pitfalls. I am hopeless, I am a loser, I am failure, I will make a fool of myself leads to feelings of worthlessness, lack of control, loss of self-esteem.	Labeling traps you. A setback is only temporary. Because someone acted inconsiderately doesn't mean it was intentional or that the person will always act that way.
He is a bastard, she is a witch makes you write someone off.	
Personalizing	**Share Responsibility**
You lose your job or lover and think you're a terrible lawyer or lover.	Consider outside reasons for what happened (company downsized, lover met someone else).
It's my fault.	You are not responsible for everything your child or husband does. Would you take credit if they did something wonderful?
You feel responsible for what happens. Your child misbehaves and you think you're a lousy mother. Your husband flirts and you think you're a lousy wife.	

Source: Adapted from the work of Martin Seligman, *Learned Optimism* and *What You Can Change and What You Can't*; David D. Burns, *Feeling Good* and *The Feeling Good Handbook*; and Daniel Goleman, *Emotional Intelligence*.

As soon as you feel an emotion that makes you uncomfortable or unhappy, ask yourself: "What was I just saying to myself that made me feel this way?"

Likewise, be more mindful of when you have a pleasant emotional experience. How come? What were you thinking? Keep it in mind the next time you have an unpleasant emotional experience!

Remember: the event didn't depress you, but what you told yourself about the event did. And the more you ruminate about the event and play the negative thoughts over and over again, the worse you will feel. Distressful rumination yields only misery.

When you feel irritated, depressed, angry

Think: You have negative thoughts about the world, other people, and yourself. But you can't change the world; you can't change other people.

When you think you need others (as opposed to want others) to help you feel good, loved, worthy, useful, you inevitably will be disappointed, which leads you to feel frustrated, rejected, angry, feeling trapped, and feeling attacked.

But you can change your thoughts. Don't accept that your interpretation, anger, or condemnation is justified. Challenge your thoughts about the world, how you perceive others, and how you talk to yourself.

The trick here is to change your attention and challenge your automatic interpretation. Depression (and anxiety) usually can be traced to irrational interpretations, such as the thinking patterns we just reviewed. So when you feel bad about something, track your thoughts.

When you feel hurt, rejected, deprived

Remember:
You do not need to be accepted or loved, even though it is highly desirable that you are.

It's appropriate to feel sad or regretful if you feel rejected, frustrated, or deprived.

Question the assumptions you have made (about what others think, how catastrophic something is, that it's all your fault, and so on).

What's the evidence for these exaggerated beliefs?

If you feel worthless because you acted badly, ask yourself, Even if I acted badly, does that mean that everything about me is worthless?

Adapted from Albert Ellis, *The Essence of Rational Psychotherapy: A Comprehensive Approach to Treatment.* New York: Institute for Rational Living, 1970.

When you feel sad

"Pain is part of life and it won't last forever. Broken hearts are wrenching and of course you will feel sad, but they ultimately heal.

"Grit your teeth and let it hurt. Don't deny it, don't be overwhelmed by it. It will not last forever. One day, the pain will be gone and you will still be there."

—Rabbi Harold S. Kushner,
When Bad Things Happen to Good People

When you feel injustice, outrage at others

Where is the proof that someone who crossed you or committed an injustice is just no good?

Although it would be better if they hadn't acted that way, you can't control how others behave. Acceptance doesn't mean you like it or you are sentenced to silence. However, you can change what *you* do and how *you* respond.

Just as you can't condemn yourself as an awful person because of something you did, you can't condemn others for the same shortcomings. We are all fallible. We need to accept ourselves and our feelings and the fact that we can't change them by will. Let them be.

Adapted from Albert Ellis, *The Essence of Rational Psychotherapy: A Comprehensive Approach to Treatment.* New York: Institute for Rational Living, 1970.

TIME AND AGAIN

The human mind has the great gift of traveling among the past, present, and future. But where you dwell can either create a depressive outlook or protect you from one.

Replaying the past over and over with all your mistakes just serves to reignite the pain, the hurt, humiliation, perceived injustices, and disappointments. The past can contaminate your present and poison the future. Do you really benefit from ruminating about past problems? Yes, it comes easily and may feel like second nature, but does that make it healthy or even true? Remember, your past can no longer touch you. You can leave it. It is just what you allow it to be in your mind. Just as you can identify and revise automatic negative thoughts, *you can learn to shift your attention to the present instead whenever you become aware of dwelling in the past.*

Free yourself from the past—it doesn't have to have any power over you. In the present, you have the opportunity for a fresh start or another try. Keep your attention on the here and now, free from the baggage of past mistakes and expectations. *Then accept the current circumstance or reality and focus on what you can do now to make things better.*

If you dwell in the imagined future, you are likely to be anxious or fearful, but the future is only a figment of your imagination. It's just what you tell yourself about what it may be—you can't read the future. It's okay to plan for the future at this moment, of course, but to fret about what-ifs and dwell now about all that can go wrong in the future is unhealthy.

"Living in the past is a dull and lonely business; looking back strains the neck muscles, and causes you to bump into people not going your way."

—Edna Ferber

Yoga, Japanese Morita and Naikan therapy, Eastern philosophy, the Forum or Landmark Education, the Power of Now, Gratefulness, shamans, gurus, coaches, and cognitive therapists—all agree that the key to mental health is peace of mind. Call it enlightenment or whatever else, it is brought about by realizing that:

- the only reality in life is the present moment;
- both the past and the future are reflections of your interpretations and imagination; they are not real;
- you don't have to believe or dwell on the thoughts that drift through your mind;
- you should become aware of your thoughts; keep your attention on the moment;
- you should accept the present circumstances.

Then focus on what the external reality calls for you to do next.

How you view the present will strongly influence your mood, motivation, resilience, and ability to take risks. Imagine the chances of successful problem solving if you believe "Why bother? Nothing I can do will help." *Remember*: The only thing you can really control is your distorted negative thinking and your behavior at the moment. The key to feeling good is to behave in your best interest now, at this moment.

Living in the present

"Only one person in a thousand knows the trick of really living in the present.

"Most of us spend fifty-nine minutes an hour living in the past, with regret for lost joys or shame for things badly done (both utterly useless and weakening).

"Or in a future which we either long for or dread.

"There is only one minute in which you are alive, this minute, here and now.

"The only way to live is by accepting each minute as an unrepeatable minute, which is exactly what it is: a miracle and unrepeatable."

—Storm Jameson

THERE NOT HERE

If you have a fight at home, leave it there. If you have an argument with your boss, leave it there. Don't let anger and frustration from home or work contaminate your mood. You don't willfully bring garbage into your home, why bring negativity and pessimism in from someplace else? Learn to relax—to let it be. Although anger can motivate problem solving, it's unlikely to do so when vented at an innocent bystander. Learn to deal with anger just like sadness. Become aware of the feeling, and identify the automatic thoughts. Look for distortions or exaggerations, examine the evidence. Suggest more rational alternatives. Practice ways of blunting the intensity of the feeling state. Sometimes the simple count-slowly-to-10 strategy is all that's needed.

WHEN YOU FEEL GUILTY

What can you learn from your guilt? It serves an important function, like a self-policeman, to help make sure that we "pull our weight" and don't let others down. You might feel guilty because you didn't bring a gift, you didn't stop by, you didn't help, you didn't contribute. But beating yourself up over what you did wrong or what you should have done is useless. Does such punishment fit the crime? Change your thoughts.

Be clear on what is *your* responsibility—and your respond-ability—and what is not. Also, ask yourself: Is someone trying to manipulate you into using your well-known talent and making you feel guilty? Remember—you can't directly change what someone else does. Maybe trying to make you feel guilty is the only way that someone knows how to ask for your help. Perhaps someone has had so much success using guilt to influence your actions that he or she doesn't have any reason to try other problem-solving strategies. Learn to use guilt rather than be used by it. Frequently we feel guilty when we have done something wrong, when we have behaved poorly. Rather than berating yourself, what can you do to offset the problem? Can you make amends? Understand your actions: Are there mitigating circumstances? What can be done differently in the future? Responding to these questions will make you feel better.

WHEN YOU'RE DRIVEN TO BE PERFECT

Perfectionism stems from all or nothing, black-and-white thinking. You set exceptionally high standards for yourself (would they be that high for your best friend?), usually because you're terrified of failing. By doing it perfectly, you'll be insulated from criticism. You think you have to earn your self-respect and need to be highly successful for others to respect or love you. But even if you live up to your high standards, chances are you still won't feel satisfied. If you don't live up to them, you will view yourself as a total failure (more all-or-nothing thinking). Who do you know who really is perfect at all things all the time?

Turn this kind of thinking around by trying these techniques:

- Go for the gold when you are charged by enthusiasm and seek the exhilaration of the sport, activity, or creative process.
- Allow yourself to feel good about your accomplishments. Pat yourself on the back, don't whip yourself.
- Since you love and respect others regardless of their success, you can relax knowing that others can love and respect you even if you aren't the best, smartest, or richest.
- If you encounter failure, acknowledge that no one can win every time. Turn the defeat into an opportunity for learning, reassessment, and growth.
- If you collect evidence that indicates that the failure was largely your fault, examine the components of the task. Not enough practice? Allowed too little time? Underestimated the difficulty? Could have used more help?

Giving up perfectionism does not equal being an indifferent slob or a big loser (again, all-or-nothing thinking). In fact, it can result in more productivity and bigger successes.

WHEN YOU FEEL RESENTMENT

Resentment is the mirror image of guilt; it occurs when you have expectations of others that aren't met. But remember, you can't directly change other people, you can only give them opportunity and feedback. Do you feel the need to control others as part of your way to try to have control over your life? In an effort to feel in control, many people develop demanding schedules and regimens to avoid feeling anxious and depressed. But what gives those people the right to demand that someone else do the same? Remember that you usually can't make other people do things and sometimes you have to accept others' decisions, even though you may not like them at all.

If you really want control, control your own responses. You'll feel better. As Gerold Jampolsky writes in *Love Is Letting Go of Fear,* "We change the world we see by changing our thoughts about it. . . . I can see the world differently by changing my mind about what I want to see."

Do What Would Help You to Feel Better

Have you ever noticed that when you feel crummy you usually don't do what is in your best interests? When you take purposeful actions and behave in ways that work toward your goals and are proactive, though, you can't help but feel better. You have a sense of purpose, a good feeling that a job is getting done, a sense of well-being, and you feel in control of life. Research proves that if you change your behavior—*whether you feel like it or not*—you will almost always feel better as a result. On the other hand, if you wait until you feel like it or feel up to it, you may end up waiting eternally.

YOU ARE WHAT YOU DO

The next step after recognizing your feelings and thoughts is to change self-sabotaging and emotionally based behaviors. *Remember*: Accept your feelings, whatever they are; view them as separate from who you are and what you identify with as a person. Recognize that it doesn't matter what you feel like doing or what's happened in the past. *What matters now is learning how to control your behaviors despite your feelings and deciding to put your attention instead on what you do in the next moment.* The more you ruminate and focus on negativity, the more negative and pessimistic you become. Grab that attention that's ruminating and tell yourself to think instead about:

What are the consequences for others of the behavior you are considering?

What needs to be done now?

What do you have to do for a more desirable outcome?

Of course, it's easier to do nothing. That's part of the definition of depression—a decrease in goal-directed behavior. You're tired, apathetic, or bored; nothing interests you much. But the longer you do nothing, the harder it gets to do something.

Just by doing a little or changing your behavior a bit, you will start to feel better and begin to recoup your self-esteem and sense of purpose. Do what you know would make you feel better if you were in the mood. This doesn't mean fake or pretend, but to *behave purposefully— just one small step at a time*. Since you can't control other people's behavior, take advantage of the power you have to control *your* behavior. You will be amazed how emotionally relieved you will be after completing even a small goal or tackling some long-avoided task.

By understanding the difference between your feelings and your actions—just because you feel angry doesn't mean you have to act out that anger—and disputing and challenging distorted negative thinking, you can behave differently. Knowing that you can always respond in your best interest is the essence of self-worth and self-respect. You need not be held hostage to emotionally based behaviors. You can respond in your best interest. When you know and behave this way, you actually open yourself to a far richer emotional life.

"When your attention is fixed on behaving constructively, your emotions won't be such a big deal to you. You'll find that in spite of how you happen to feel at the moment, you will be able to accomplish what you have set out to do. . . . We change only by changing the now. That is all we have to work with. What I *do* now is me and molds who I will become tomorrow. . . .

We are responsible for what we do no matter how we feel at the time."

—David K. Reynolds, *Constructive Living*

Or as psychologist Martin Seligman puts it: "Once a depressed person becomes active and hopeful, self-esteem always improves."

To Feel Better

No rationalizations, just reason.

Accept the reality.

Accept your feelings. (You can't always be happy.)

Listen to your thoughts.
 (Using the skills above. What would you tell a friend who was recycling your thoughts?)

Consider what you can control (your behavior) and what you can't control (almost everything else).

Identify your purpose and make a small, manageable goal.

Then do something (what the reality calls for) toward that goal *whether you feel like it or not.*

Then do the next thing that needs to be done.

Don't wait until you feel like it. Once you get started, your feelings will follow your behaviors and you will feel like it.
 When dealing with others: put yourself in their shoes and consider the impact your behavior has on them.

When you think, "I wish I weren't so (tired, miserable, sad, etc.)," reframe it as, "I am glad that at least I . . . I certainly am (tired, miserable, sad). But I can do a little." Or, "The sooner I do something, the better, so just do it." Or, "It would be better for me if I were to . . ." Or, "What needs to be done next?"

Do it

When you say, I can't . . .
 break off this abusive relationship
 quit this job that makes me unhappy
 tell him that . . .

What you really mean is, "I'm afraid to . . . I have never in the past . . ."

When you say, I should, but I don't want to . . .
 get out of bed
 take on this huge task
 get exercise . . .

give yourself a small, manageable, and realistic task purposely directed to achieving your goal.

Then, do it.

Let's look at a typical situation and apply these principles. For example, let's say you lose your job. Your first automatic thought probably will be "This is the worst thing that could happen. I am a failure, a loser. I will never find a job as good as that one. Why does this always happen to me?" Instead, apply the thought and behavior principles discussed so far.

Identify the distorted thoughts

You have made it a catastrophe (you're not going to die). You are seeing it as black and white and are generalizing the problem to every aspect of your life, calling yourself a failure or loser. You're not going to be jobless forever, so don't view it as permanent doom or a forecast of the future, much less the worst possible future. Don't be a victim of your automatic thoughts.

Dispute your thinking

Where's the evidence that you are worthless? That you will never find another good job? What would you tell a friend in your situation? Look for the gray, rather than putting everything in black and white, all or nothing.

Accept your feelings

It's appropriate to feel sad, a sense of loss, hurt, ashamed that you are out of work.

Focus on what to do

What needs to be done next? Even though you don't feel like it, identify what you know you would feel good about doing. Put your attention on taking one small step toward that goal. In the case of unemployment, put your resume together, make five calls a day, contact the unemployment or job service office. Rather than fret, tell yourself to think about what you might do next instead. Constructive, positive, well-thought-out action.

Accept What You Can't Change

May you
accept the things you cannot change,
have the courage to change the things you can change,
and the wisdom to know the difference.

—adapted from the Serenity Prayer, attributed to Friedrich Oestinger and to Reinhold Neibuhr; used by 12-step programs around the world.

ADD FUN AND FLOW

Do not stay in bed longer than your usual waking time and do not take naps. To feel better, engage in activities that relax you and bring you pleasure. Although drugs or alcohol can be a source of pleasure, they can actually promote or worsen depression.

Remember what activities used to bring you joy, feelings of self-worth, or a sense of well-being? Make time to pursue these activities more often, *whether you feel like it or not*. These may be as simple as going to an aerobics class, a movie, a concert, getting a massage, sketching by a lake, working in the garden, writing in a journal, playing tennis or golf, etc. They may not boost your mood a lot at first, but they are almost always better than doing nothing. Try to enhance them by savoring them—review them in your mind, detail the specific pleasures, build a memory from it, share it with others. We'll detail more relaxation strategies in chapter 10.

Remember: when you're alone and inactive, it's almost certain that you will think about your difficulties and will feel worse. Distraction may be a low tech way of managing your low moods, but it is reliable.

Even more powerful than distracting activities, however, are the activities in which you forget yourself, your problems, and the time, and you enter into what some call a state of flow. You become so immersed in what you're doing that you lose all self-consciousness or sense of self. Depressed people are always thinking about their sad and gloomy feelings, but people in flow are too absorbed to think about themselves or their feelings. Activities that trigger the state of flow are those in which you are actively involved, you have a sense of mastery or control over, and you forget yourself. The more flow in your life, the more it will fortify you psychologically.

Related to fun and flow is some intriguing preliminary research that suggests that the act of smiling may improve mood. Even if you have to force yourself to smile, the facial movements may influence your emotions. It may be one more behavior that, whether you feel like it or not, will make you feel better. It certainly can't make you feel worse.

Activity schedule

To ensure fun and pleasure, keep a chart of how many activities you engage in each day that are either fun, pleasurable, or give you a sense of mastery. Be sure you have at least several a day!

Your well-being should be high on your priority list; don't assume you'd never have the time.

Strategies that work

Not sure what to do first to feel better? Try these strategies.

- Know your priorities and take things one at a time.
- Break big jobs into small ones, one small task at a time.
- Keep goals small and short term.
- Get some exercise.
- Don't wait to feel better to behave better—do it.

HELP OTHERS

Researchers also find that people's moods usually improve when they do something to help others (volunteer work, kindness to a neighbor, visit to a nursing home, pick up some litter, hold a door open). It not only distracts you from your own problems but makes you feel better because you have done something worthwhile.

BE MINDFUL AND GRATEFUL

To be mindful means to pay sharper attention to the present, to observe as much as possible about the present moment without judging, reflecting, or thinking, and to have no opinions or no interpretation about whether it's pleasant or unpleasant. You are just alert to the moment and your surroundings.

So often we go through life with our minds buzzing, mindless of the moment or world around. The goal of mindfulness is to be super-aware of the moment without distraction. By stopping yourself from evaluating every detail as sad, irritable, embarrassing, shameful, and so on, you stop your inner voice from nagging and become more open to the moment.

Being grateful is an attitude, and its practice of noticing life, goodness, truth, and beauty is at the heart of every religion and spiritual tradition. Gratefulness is a virtue that prompts an increased sense of well-being and a desire to do good in the world. One simple way to practice gratefulness is to reflect on the past 24 hours and identify those things for which you are grateful and awed. Being mindful of gratefulness helps put you in a more appreciative and beneficent state of mind, countering the habit of talking to yourself in a negative and pessimistic manner.

When Troubled Relationships
Darken Your World

How can you feel loving and loved without positive and trusting personal relationships? If you don't have a strong social support network, it's easy to become socially isolated, lonely, withdrawn, and probably self-deprecating. On the other hand, if you learn basic social skills that foster a strong network of loving relationships, you can make it through stress, loss, and disappointment unscathed by dysthymia or depression.

Maintaining close, positive, and trusting interpersonal relationships is critical for mental health and for relieving depressive symptoms. Recent studies show, for example, that women with dysthymia have poor social skills and have had them for years. They tend to be much less comfortable with social interaction, tend to avoid eye contact and social contact, and have fewer friends than women who are not depressed. Moreover, dysthymic women in these studies had significantly lower incomes and smaller living spaces than those who did not have dysthymia (another reason to address your dysthymia!). Without putting into motion a plan of action, it is likely that these women will remain socially isolated, have little or no social support, have little or no social life, and feel rejected, lonely, sad, and bereft.

Yet numerous studies show that when dysthymic or depressed people learn, often through therapy, better social skills and strategies to improve their relationships, their gloomy sad moods significantly lift and they are better prepared to tackle their life problems.

We tend to use the same types of distorted thinking patterns described above in our interpersonal relationships. When we get angry or hurt or frustrated with others, we tend to assault the other's character by overgeneralizing and labeling ("You are so selfish or careless or rude or . . ."), rather than staying focused on the specific problem. Here are some tips to break the pattern.

- Catch yourself making judgments or attacking thoughts (they're often automatic thoughts) about others.
- Let go of all grudges and grievances from the past and stick to the present.
- Learn to forgive—both yourself and others. Giving an offender the gift of forgiveness is an unselfish act, but you directly benefit: it frees you from being controlled by bitterness or resentment from a past injustice. You are no longer a victim but can derive a sense of peace.
- Ask for forgiveness.

- Lower your expectations of others. Remember: We can't control others but have to accept what they choose to do.
- Learn how to express your feelings without acting on them; control your impulses.
- Manage conflict by showing you are hearing the other person by repeating what you believe the other person is trying to say, is feeling, and is thinking.
- Empathize with the other person.
- Prevent escalation; stay calm.
- Offer concrete solutions.

And, perhaps most important, realize that other people don't have to change for you, even if you choose noncritical, nonattacking comments.

Dealing with Others

Here are how the distorted thinking patterns can interfere with good communication and interpersonal relations and how to remedy them. Study them carefully as they are the keys to promoting positive relationships.

Distorted Communication	Constructive Communication
ABC	**XYZ**
You	Be very specific without attacking
Attack	one's character (and use I state-
Blame	ments): I feel X when you do Y,
Criticize	and if you could maybe instead
	do Z in that kind of situation, I
	wouldn't feel this way.
Right or Wrong	**Describe the Problem without**
He has no right . . .	**Judgment**
You were wrong to . . .	Describe your feelings about what
It's your fault that . . .	happened and consider that it
Constructive criticism is really an	can be different next time:
attack—you're trying to show	He really hurt me when he . . .
you're right and they're wrong.	I felt rejected or unloved when you
To prove to yourself that you're	left me in the lurch . . .
right about your assumptions,	Well, it's unfortunate that this has
you keep looking for evidence to	happened; now what can we do?
confirm your underlying	Do you want to be right or do you
assumptions. You become	want to be happy?
convinced that the other person	
is flawed and unchangeable.	

Distorted Communication	Constructive Communication
Jumping to Conclusions You assume the worse, most negative explanation for something. Someone's late: you write them off as inconsiderate or selfish, wasting your time. Someone yawns while you're talking: you assume they're rude, think you are stupid. Someone doesn't call: you resent them, get angry. "My husband wouldn't understand . . ." You're convinced your interpretation is right. This leads to lower self-esteem, anger, resentment.	**Consider the Possibilities** Maybe the person got held up in traffic Maybe they didn't sleep well last night. Maybe they had to work or help a relative. Give others the benefit of the doubt. Don't be a fortuneteller: don't assume that you know how someone else will respond; don't assume that you will be a failure at something.
Name-calling or Labeling Attacks You assault someone's character instead of their behavior: 　You are so selfish or irrational or inconsiderate or controlling or stubborn or insensitive . . . 　You are such a slob . . . 　You are an ass, jerk. . . . 　You just went ahead and . . . 　You didn't . . . 　You have no right to . . .	**Describe Problem Behavior Instead with I statements** I wish I could have some help with . . . I got so frustrated when the house was such a mess and . . . I felt betrayed when . . . I felt like I had no say when . . . I feel rejected or unloved or ignored or coerced or hurt . . . I was hurt or sad or disappointed or nervous when . . . I feel frustrated or angry or uncomfortable when . . .
Your Shoes You see everything from your point of view only: 　I can't believe he ignored me! 　He hated my proposal but I worked so hard on it and he just disregarded my ideas!	**Their Shoes** Imagine what it might be like for them? Empathize with the other person's feelings: 　Maybe he had his mind on work problems . . . 　Maybe I didn't understand what he needed for that proposal . . . 　She's under a lot of pressure and my project didn't help her . . .

(*continues*)

Distorted Communication	Constructive Communication
Sarcasm, Mockery, Insult, Hostility, Disgust	**Keep Voice Calm and Normal, Accept Feelings, and Try to Give a Positive Response**

You mock the other person by mimicking him or her.
    Yeah, right, I'm sure you . . .
    Hah!
    Go to hell!
	I can understand why you are so angry. You thought I . . .
	I have a lot of respect for the way that you . . .
	We're both angry, but I know we can work it out together . . .

Defensiveness When Attacked	**Acknowledge the Complaint; Find Some Truth in It**

You think I'm sloppy or inconsiderate or lazy! What about when you . . .
I am not! I did this or that!
That's not true!
That's ridiculous!
You're the one who said . . .
	Rephrase what was said. This shows you are trying to understand their frustration or anger and to respect their feelings. Such acknowledgment is very healing for the other person:
	    I can see you're disappointed in my project.
	    Let me see if I understand . . .
	    You sound really angry and you're right—I sometimes do get too . . .
	    I know you're upset because I am often late, lazy, overreact, or don't help you enough . . .
	    I understand that you were hurt when . . .
	    It sounds like you feel . . .is that right?

Mind Reading	**No One Can Mind Read**
I didn't ask you because you always, never think, or hate it when . . . You resent it when I . . .	You can't know what others think and feel so don't even try. Likewise, express your feelings (with I statements) and what's on your mind since others can't know.

Distorted Communication	Constructive Communication
Angry Behaviors Slamming doors Throwing dishes Giving the silent treatment Being rude Pouting	**Don't *Act* on Your Feelings, State Them; Ask Gently about Others' Feelings and Thoughts** Are you angry at me because I . . . Are you feeling hurt because . . . Please tell me what you didn't like about . . .
Mental Filtering A bad thing happens with another person and you start to look for that flaw and other flaws again and again, overlooking the good points or kind actions.	**Keep Glasses Neutral, Don't Ruminate** View the problem as something that happened but that can be different next time.
Disqualifying the Positive He brought me flowers, gave me a massage, wrote a nice note, but that's because he felt so guilty, just wants to get on my good side . . .	**Enjoy and Believe the Positive** Acknowledge the kindness, the gesture. I was so angry with him last week but this gesture was really kind or took a lot of courage, was really nice . . .
Trying to Change Others You should . . . I wish you would . . . Why can't you . . . Much of our distress with others stems from trying to change them by constructive criticism, saying they should do this or that, trying to prove they're wrong (we're right), etc. This makes others defensive and critical of us.	**Accept Others** By accepting others, even with all their weaknesses, without demands and expectations, you not only stay calm but aren't attacking them in any way. They, in turn, won't be defensive and continue the spiral of attacks and discord.

Source: Adapted from the work of Martin Seligman, *Learned Optimism* and *What You Can Change and What You Can't*; David D. Burns, *Feeling Good* and *The Feeling Good Handbook*; and Daniel Goleman, *Emotional Intelligence*

People with dysthymia tend to be passive. Often, they cling to a relationship that in fact is not working for them because they feel too insecure or inadequate to do anything about it. A psychotherapist can help people explore their troublesome relationships and explore such questions as:

- Why is the relationship gratifying to you? Or is it? Would you be better off without it?
- What does the other person get from you? Are your values and expectations about the same?
- What are your options in terms of the relationship? Should it be renegotiated? Ended?
- Does the other person know how you feel? Do you know how to express your feelings?
- Is the relationship contributing to your depressive outlook (feelings of helplessness, irritability, hopelessness, sadness)?

Comments from Constructive Living

You can't build a life on feeling good all the time.

Insight or self-understanding often is not enough to offer a way out of difficulty; action is usually necessary, as well.

The optimal mind isn't peaceful or blissful; it is flexible, adapting to changing circumstances.

Feelings don't need to be fixed.

You don't need to fight against your fears.

Fears are just fine as they are. They provide useful information.

What I did just now is already past.

Whether that moment brought success or failure,

The next moment is now arriving.

Herein lies existential hope—not as a feeling, but as an integral part of reality.

—David Reynolds, author of *Constructive Living*

Reprinted with permission.

Next, we'll discuss the types of psychotherapies that can relieve dysthymia when you just can't turn your own negativity and pessimism around by yourself.

6

◆ ◆ ◆

Psychotherapy

I know of no
More encouraging fact
Than the unquestionable ability of man
to elevate his life by a conscious endeavor.

—Henry David Thoreau

In the depth of winter,
I finally learned that within me
There lay in an invincible summer.

—Albert Camus

How Do You Know If You Need Professional Help?

Consider seeking professional help when you recognize that you are unhappy—lonely, depressed, anxious, agitated, distressed over difficult relationships at work and at home, stuck in your life, losing ground, losing your enthusiasm, giving up more and more often, feeling helpless and passive. A good time to seek professional help is when you wish you felt more vital and alive, more joyful and purposeful, and less down all the time.

Before active therapies were available, people didn't have the opportunities we have today to learn how to change their outlook on life but had to accept their view of the world as normal. This situation is analogous to life before the invention of glasses. You usually could get by, but life was often out of focus and much more difficult to cope with, yet normal. Normal swiftly changed, however, to 20/20 as soon as glasses were invented.

Some 80 percent of those with dysthymia report significant relief with treatment, astonished that they have lived their whole lives under the pessimistic gloomy cloud of dysthymia, not knowing what feeling good felt like. So would you choose now not to wear glasses or see the world as sharply as possible?

If you believe you have dysthymia, seek professional help. You will be surprised at how much better you will feel. The best treatments for dysthymia are various types of psychotherapy and antidepressants, either alone or in combination.

Where should you start? Here are a few general guidelines.

Consider medication if:

- You can't reap *any* pleasure out of your daily life
- You have tried medication in the past and it has helped
- One or more family members has had a good response to medication
- The depression is becoming more and more severe, even disabling

In these cases, you may have chemical imbalances based on genetic inheritances; antidepressant medication may be a good place to start.

Consider psychotherapy first if:

- You believe your suffering stems from life's problems and outside stresses
- You have suffered a significant recent loss or trauma or other psychosocial problems
- You hate the idea of taking medication

Studies at the University of Pittsburgh Medical Center also suggest that people who are depressed but sleep normally may be more responsive to psychotherapy. Those with sleep problems seem to respond better to medication.

In recent years, the treatment of dysthymia has gone through a major transformation, with antidepressant medications taking the lead role in treatment options, while talk therapy or psychotherapy is losing ground. To some extent, this reflects new evidence establishing that various antidepressants are effective treatments of chronic, mild depressions. There is no clinical evidence to support this bias. This chapter on psychotherapy and the next on medication can inform you of what to expect from both psychotherapy and pharmaceutical treatment of dysthymia and mild depression.

How Successful Is Psychotherapy?

Certain styles of psychotherapy are just as effective as medication in relieving dysthymia, according to various studies. Cognitive-behavioral therapy and interpersonal psychotherapy, in particular, work extremely well because they are short-term therapies (8 to 12 weeks) that don't dwell on the past but focus on the here and now with an eye on the future. With a few months of either psychotherapy or medication, you have a 50 percent chance of full recovery. Combining both treatments, your odds of full relief jump to 85 percent.

Even just a few sessions with a good therapist can help. According to one study, for example, three sessions of cognitive-behavioral therapy and interpersonal psychotherapy helped 75 percent of the time for low-level chronic depression, and the relief persisted even a year later, especially among those who had cognitive-behavioral therapy.

That's extraordinarily successful treatment. Yet, only one in five people with dysthymia actually seek help, largely because of their defeatist, negative attitude that it probably won't work anyway. How wrong they are.

How Therapy Helps

Sharing feelings, sorrows, and problems with a therapist you trust and respect can bring enormous emotional relief. However, because dwelling on the past, searching for unconscious motivations, or blaming your parents may not help people shed the cloak of dysthymia, a skilled therapist instead can show you how your style of thinking, your social skills, and your coping strategies contribute to your depressive way of life and how to change them.

The primary goal isn't to help you feel better, but to help you respond better. A side effect of behaving better is you *feel* better.

These practically oriented therapies that are showing success in combating dysthymia (and other forms of chronic depression) are becoming more popular as their effectiveness becomes more widely recognized. They also can be less expensive than long-term analytic and other insight-oriented therapies that seek to change character as the treatment period is much shorter—8 to 12 weeks to learn and practice the strategies and to recognize and change self-defeating thinking and behavior.

In addition to the education involved, psychotherapy also may help because it can actually change the biology of the brain in similar ways to medication. This makes sense if you think about how therapy can help reduce anxiety and its accompanying stress hormone levels. Also, studies using EEGs (sleep electroencephalograms) show that the brains in people for whom psychotherapy was successful exhibit the same biological changes as those of people who feel better due to medication.

Benefits of psychotherapy

- No side effects
- Benefits persist long after treatment ends (unlike medication)
- Emotional relief from the reassurance from a professional that your problem is highly treatable
- New skills to prevent future problems
- Empathy from a warm, caring, and skilled clinician
- Optimism for the future

The psychotherapies described below overlap a great deal. What they have in common is their short-term course of treatment and their focus on the present and on styles of thinking and coping. Unlike psychoanalysis or psychodynamic therapy that would explore how the dysthymia was triggered by childhood experiences and was internalized as conflicts among the id, ego, and superego or was due to repressed impulses, these strategies look for negative and irrational thinking patterns.

Cognitive-BehavioralTherapy	*Interpersonal Therapy*	*Problem-solving Therapy*
Focuses on how style of self-talk, automatic thoughts, and behavior affect others. Teaches new styles of thinking, coping skills, and shows how action provides emotional relief.	Focuses on resolving interpersonal conflicts and expanding social support network. Boosts self-esteem.	Focuses on identifying areas in your life that are causing distress.
Reduces feelings of helplessness	*Strengthens interpersonal relationships*	*Strengthens coping strategies*

Choosing a Therapist

The most important aspect of therapy is the skill of the therapist. One of the most important traits to look for in a therapist is warmth and a sense of connection with that person so that you feel you are understood. Unlike the classical stereotype of a neutral therapist who may at times seem uncaring and aloof, it's important that you can easily talk to this person and that you sense the therapist cares about you. It may take visits to several therapists to find one you feel comfortable with.

It's less important whether the therapist is a clinical social worker, psychologist, or psychiatrist as long as your insurance approves of the licensure of your therapist, you feel connected to the therapist, and the therapist has experience with dysthymia, preferably from a cognitive, behavioral, or interpersonal point of view.

Psychotherapists and Dysthymia		
Degree	**Title**	**Education/Experience**
M.D.	psychiatrist	Medical degree, 8 years or more of postcollege training. Usually, the only kind of therapist who can prescribe medication.
Ph.D., Psy.D., or Ed.D.	psychologist	Doctoral-level degree. May or may not have a clinical license.
M.S.W. L.M.S.W. (licensed), A.C.S.W (accredited),	social worker	Two years of graduate training
C.S.W. (certified)	social worker	Two years of graduate training plus special clinical experience or higher level exams.
Not Necessarily Recommended for Dysthymia		
	psychoanalyst	Training in psychoanalysis, a style of therapy which is not particularly useful for the treatment of dysthymia.

You might start by getting referrals from a county or community mental health center or from your physician. In addition to inquiring about cost, insurance coverage, and availability, you might ask your potential therapists these questions.

- What type of psychotherapeutic approach do you use? Do you focus on my past or on my current problems?

   Look for cognitive, behavioral, and interpersonal approaches. How you are coping now rather than what caused your problems in the past, should be the focus.

- How long is a typical course of treatment for dysthymia?

   Look for short-term therapy: weekly, from 8 to 24 visits.

- What's your experience with dysthymia?

   Look for someone who knows what dysthymia is and has helped other people with similar problems get better.

- What's the rationale for the treatment of dysthymia?

   Look for someone who looks at attitudes, thought patterns, and activities at the root of chronic depression.

- As a therapist, do you believe in staying neutral and waiting for me to find insights or are you directive?

   Look for someone who will be active and willing to teach and guide you to overcome apathy, passivity, and helplessness.

- What if you need medication?

   Look for someone who has a working relationship with a psychiatrist, or try a psychiatrist first.

You are looking for someone to help you monitor your thinking patterns and explanatory style to change your tendencies to think in self-defeating, depressive ways and to help you change your behavior so you will feel in more control of it and work toward improving your situation.

WHAT TO SAY

Bring to your visit a list of:

- Your psychological symptoms, including irritability, inability to make decisions or to concentrate, etc. (see symptoms of dysthymia and depression in chapter 2, but don't limit your symptoms to this list)

- Physical symptoms, including fatigue, aches and pains, back pain, headaches, stomach problems, sleep and eating habits, or problems with libido

- Severity of each of the symptoms

- Length of time that you been feeling this way; when did you first notice the problem

- Any medical illnesses or medications you take, including supplements, birth controls pills, hormone replacement therapy, etc.

- A timetable of your most stressful life events

If possible, bring a mood diary (see page 165).

Cognitive-Behavioral Therapy

Cognitive-behavioral therapy focuses on learning how to recognize automatic, pessimistic patterns of thinking, faulty perceptions, unrealistic expectations, irrational interpretations, catastrophic thinking, and the critical self-talk that created the dysthymia in the first place. If you often say to yourself, "I'm a loser," or, "everything happens to me," or, "this will never change," or, "nothing goes my way," or, "I can't . . . ," then you may have fallen into automatic distorted thinking patterns.

Through therapy, you learn how your mood comes from your thoughts and your explanatory style, and how when your thoughts recycle the same negative views, you not only come to take these thoughts as gospel but they pull you down and demoralize you. With practice, you learn to screen your thoughts for negative assumptions you've made (probably for years), such as all-or-nothing thinking (see chapter 5) and to weigh the evidence for or against them. As you learn to control your pessimistic thinking, your depressive symptoms are likely to fade. You come to recognize which kinds of problems *can* be changed and that need to just be accepted. Then you practice constructive and behavior- or action-oriented thinking.

In therapy, you may have homework to practice identifying and challenging irrational thoughts and developing new skills, and you may be asked to keep a journal or diary. You may agree with the therapist to try certain activities or actions that may make you feel better and to test whether your self-defeating thoughts are valid or not.

	Comparing Styles of Recommended Therapy		
Approach	Cognitive Behavioral Therapy (CBT)	Interpersonal Therapy (IPT)	Problem-solving Therapy
Emphases	Current thoughts	Current relationships	Current coping
Time focus Time plan for therapy	Look at the present Short-term	Look at the present Short-term	Look at the present Short-term
Structure	Examine how self-defeating thoughts cause unhappiness	Examine how interpersonal problems cause unhappiness	Examine current problems and generate solutions
Skills	Learn new ways of thinking	Learn interpersonal skills	Learn new ways of coping
Goal	Change habitual ways of thinking that bring you down	Practical successes: solve problems to achieve sense of well-being	To solve problems, achieve goals, and change behavior
	Hope, optimism Mastery, self-assertion	Hope, optimism Mastery, self-assertion	

Interpersonal Therapy (IPT)

Whereas cognitive-behavioral therapy seems particularly useful for people who brood a lot, interpersonal therapy might be most beneficial for people with dysthymic disorder who have had very difficult lives. IPT views dysthymia as a medical illness and focuses on how recent events and the relationships in your life are connected to mood and depressive symptoms.

The therapist would help you see that when bad things happen, it's not necessarily your fault but part of life's hard knocks and that your expectations may be inappropriate; just as in cognitive-behavioral therapy, the therapist would encourage you to pursue activities that would help you feel better.

Although you may explore where your problems took root in childhood (such as trauma or loss), the focus stays on your symptoms and current problems in life, particularly social and family problems. IPT focuses on four problem areas that you may work on improving: communication skills, coping with major life changes, processing grief, and expanding social connections.

GRIEF AND LOSS

If you have suffered a severe loss, such as the loss of a child, your health, your job, or your independence because of a caregiving role, for example, the therapist would help you to move through the process of grief, to recognize how the loss has contributed to your depressive symptoms and how you may be idealizing the loss, and generally to explore both the positive and negative aspects of the loss.

ROLE DISPUTE

When conflicts persist with a spouse, child, parent, boss, co-worker, or sibling, a person with dysthymia may blame herself and feel unworthy and fearful of losing the relationship. The therapist would help examine whether the relationship is gratifying enough to salvage or if you are merely sticking with it because you feel inadequate and are scared of letting go. You might explore such questions as, What do you hope to get out of this relationship? Are your expectations and values similar or very different from the other person's? Do you have the option to redefine or terminate the relationship? Are you adequately expressing your anger? guilt? resentment? How is the relationship contributing to your depressive symptoms? And you will probably develop some strategies to resolve the relationship.

ROLE TRANSITION

IPT views some cases of dysthymia as stemming from the stress of major upheavals in life—such as having a baby, getting a new job, moving to a new city, having a new illness—that has resulted in a sense of chaos, hopelessness, pining for the past when everything was predictable, and viewing the present and future as horrible. The therapist might help you to see the good sides of the transition while acknowledging the bad sides, to recognize the reality of the losses and how to grieve them appropriately while recognizing the limitations of the old situation. Throughout this process, a goal would be for you to view the current problem or new stage of life as an opportunity for growth and to explore how to regain a sense of control over life.

INTERPERSONAL SKILL DEFICITS

IPT, like cognitive therapy, also focuses on strengthening social skills to prevent or relieve social isolation. The therapist would help you recognize that feelings of low self-esteem or shyness are the effects of the dysthymia rather than facts of life and would help you manage or reframe anxiety and anger and explore ways to be more social via activities, hobbies, etc. You might practice assertiveness skills, how to express anger constructively, how to cope with current problems, and how to let go of the past with its gourd of grudges.

Other Promising Therapies

Problem-solving therapy (PST) and cognitive-behavioral analysis system of psychotherapy (CBASP), which are not as widely practiced as CBT or IPT, also focus on the present and current problems in the context of social relationships.

In PST, you and the therapist work together to resolve conflicts and problems, to identify and work toward goals, and to change self-defeatist styles of behavior. Typically, therapists will use a concrete step-by-step strategy to solve problems:

- Define the problem
- Identify your goals
- Generate possible solutions
- Choose the best option
- Implement that plan
- Assess the effects

CBASP is a blend of various approaches and is the only system developed especially for dysthymia and other chronic depressive disorders. The therapist teaches a formal set of steps in how to look at social problems and interact empathetically with others by showing you the consequences of your behavior on your environment. Viewing the dysthymia as a failure to cope well with life's setbacks, the therapist focuses on showing you how to identify what the consequences of your behavior might be. That insight informs your choice of behavior.

Although psychotherapy for dysthymia is most commonly done with an individual, those with dysthymia can also benefit from working in groups to practice identifying and challenging faulty perceptions.

A family approach may help to resolve persistent family conflicts and to help other members of the family also recognize and practice cognitive strategies.

Next, we'll look at turning to professionals for biochemical help and the medications for dysthymia.

7

♦ ♦ ♦

Medications

We try a new drug, a new combination
of drugs, and suddenly
I fall into my life again

like a vole picked up by a storm
then dropped three valleys
and two mountains away from home.
I can find my way back. I know. . . .

—Jane Kenyon, *Otherwise: New & Selected Poems*

Drug therapy hacks through the vines. You can feel it
happening, how the medication seems to be poisoning the
parasite so that bit by bit it withers away . . .

—Andrew Solomon, *The Noonday Demon*

If you have dysthymia, how do you know when or whether you should take an antidepressant medication? Here are some guidelines. Definitely consider medication if:

- You've had at least 2 major episodes of major depression in the past
- You've taken antidepressants before and they've been helpful
- You have a family history of depression
- You know you don't want to try to help yourself or to seek therapy
- You are severely depressed: you have suicidal thoughts, are agitated, panicky, extremely indecisive, irritable, angry, can't get out of bed

Antidepressants work the first time they are tried about half the time. When a sequence of medication trials are used, particularly in combination with therapy, the rate of their effectiveness increases to about 80 percent.

Antidepressant Facts

Although antidepressants may be taken for years, they are not addictive. Antidepressants don't alter your perceptions the way that tranquilizers or painkillers can. Antidepressants don't make nondepressed people giddy or unusually happy. Nor do they make you feel numb to the world's woes. Rather, when antidepressants work, they simply restore your normal abilities to think and feel.

Antidepressants	
Pros	**Cons**
Safe, even if taken for a long time	Expensive
Seldom cause serious problems	Often cause side effects (at least 30% to 60% of the time), e.g., sexual dysfunction, insomnia, nausea, other gastrointestinal problems
May help more quickly than psychotherapy	Not panaceas: may take up to 12 weeks to make a difference, up to six months for full effect; there is only a 50–50 chance that the first medication you try will work
	Safety when taken during pregnancy not established

Some people may view taking an antidepressant for the treatment of dsythymia as evidence that it is a disease that has to be medicated. Although the stigma of taking antidepressants has waned dramatically in recent years, some people still feel ashamed to think they have an emotional problem and that medication is a crutch. Yet, you would be far from alone: an estimated 28 million adult Americans—one out of ten people—take antidepressants, according to the National Institute of Mental Health.

A good place to discuss these issues first are with your family doctor; among mental health professionals, psychiatrists (who are physicians) are usually the only ones who can prescribe medication.

If you've never taken an antidepressant, your doctor will probably suggest first trying a "selective serotonin reuptake inhibitor" or SSRI, such as Prozac (fluoxetine), Zoloft (sertraline), Paxil (paroxetine), Luvox (fluvoxamine), Celexa (citalopram), and Lexapro (escitalopram); there are also the "serotonin-norepinephrine reuptake inhibitors" duloxetine (Cymbalta) and venlafaxine (Effexor XR). These medications usually can be started at a low therapeutic dose and under your doctor's supervision; one or two dose increases may be tried if necessary over the next six to eight weeks (the maximum therapeutic dose). Your doctor should schedule follow-up visits every two to four weeks to monitor the medication.

Even though all of the 20 or so antidepressants available are useful medications, SSRIs are usually the first medications tried because they have far fewer side effects and are safer if taken in overdose than the older medications. The effectiveness of one SSRI seems no different from another for major depression. Although there are fewer studies on newer antidepressants and their benefit for dysthymia, more than 300 studies show that these newer antidepressants (Prozac, Zoloft, Paxil, Effexor, and Serzone), which target serotonin or norepinephrine, are effective for depression and well tolerated.

If you detect no improvement with an SSRI after six weeks, venlafaxine or a tricyclic may be prescribed. Numerous studies show that imipramine (Tofranil) and desipramine (Norpramin, Pertofrane) can help dysthymia. Or a different newer antidepressant, such as bupropion (Wellbutrin) or mirtazapine (Remeron) might be used before turning to the older medications, a tricyclic or monoamine oxidase inhibitor (MAOI).

When dysthymia is difficult to treat, many doctors recommend taking a second medication to enhance the antidepressant's effects, such as lithium, a stimulant, or a hormone (e.g., a thyroid drug). For middle-aged men and women who develop dysthymia, particularly women, a hormone treatment is sometimes just as effective as an antidepressant.

All told, more than two-thirds of those with dysthymia experience significant relief when they take medication with no other therapies, according to a number of studies.

HOW ANTIDEPRESSANTS WORK

The brain is like a buzzing hive of nerves cells shaped with multiple nerve endings that are separated from each other by small gaps called synapses. The cells communicate with each other via electrical charges that trigger the nerve endings from one cell to release chemical communicators, the neurotransmitters, so they can jump the gap between nerve cells, and attach to the next neuron. The message may continue to thread its way, riding along from one cell to the next, or it may actually trigger changes in the receiving cell. Various types of neurotransmitters carry along different types of messages.

But the nerve endings have receptors that are very specific, like locks, and each is shaped to fit one kind of molecule or neurotransmitter.

Antidepressants serve as chemical facilitators. After a cell fires, neurotransmitters are reabsorbed—this is called reuptake. The so-called selective serotonin reuptake inhibitors (SSRIs) help block that reuptake, thereby increasing the amount of serotonin available in the synapse. Most of the tricyclics are thought to relieve depression primarily by blocking the reuptake of another neurotransmitter, norepinephrine.

WHAT TO CONSIDER

When you consult for the first time with your doctor or a psychiatrist about taking an antidepressant, the physician will consider:

- Your medical and psychiatric history
- Your current medications, including any over-the-counter medications, sedatives, pain relievers, headache medications, and hormones,
- The possible side effects of an antidepressant
- The cost

Typical plan of action

- Ideally, see a therapist at the same time.
- Your doctor will start you at a low dose of antidepressant medication for several weeks to see what your response is to the medication and then increase the dose weekly up to the full standard dose.
- Keep taking medication even if you feel better.
- Don't stop the medication without first checking with your doctor; some medications have uncomfortable side effects if stopped abruptly (dizziness, headache, nausea, vomiting, diarrhea, insomnia, irritability, depressed mood, and anxiety). *They are not habit-forming, however!*
- Schedule pleasant activities as your body gets used to the medication.
- Give the medication at least a month trial, even if you experience side effects. Side effects are likely to occur before any benefits but, over time, the side effects fade as the medication becomes effective and stays effective. If you feel some benefit, an even longer trial (i.e., 8 to 12 weeks) might be needed to determine if the match between patient and medication is optimal.
- Be prepared for some trial and error: if one medication doesn't work, there's a 50–50 chance another will. Try at least two antidepressants of different classes, given at full therapeutic doses for at least a month or two each, before you consider giving up. If you're willing to try several medications, your chance of relief is about 65 percent. If you'll try up to four, your chances of relief jump to 80 percent, without any psychotherapy, according to various studies.

Don't expect

- A quick fix
- Waves of euphoria, happiness, or high energy. If any of these do happen, you could be in trouble. Up to 3 to 5 percent of people with dysthymia develop bipolar disorder (mania or hypomania) on antidepressants.

Do expect to feel

- Frustrated and demoralized if the first medication doesn't work. Not responding to one antidepressant, however, is no indication that you won't respond to another. If medication isn't working after a reasonable trial period, consider asking for a referral to psychotherapist (if you don't have one already). After several unsuccessful medication trials, ask for a referral to a psychiatrist who specializes in these medications.
- Side effects, especially the first week or so, though they are mild and may include dry mouth, stomach problems, headache, and jitteriness. The side effects of some medications are bothersome at the beginning but then taper off before the full beneficial effects of the medication occur. Long-term problems may include sexual problems and weight gain.

You can hopefully expect to experience

- A gradual lifting of sadness, worry, fatigue, and low mood, less sensitivity to rejection, more assertiveness, more socially inclined, confident, alert, and more energetic. An antidepressant that works is one that will make you feel less sluggish—both mentally and physically—and more vital
- Improvements in sleep, sense of humor, and concentration
- Increases in your doses and longer time periods for them to take effect

SIDE EFFECTS

As many as one-third of those who are treated for depression with an antidepressant don't even fill the first prescription. And about half of those who try antidepressants experience side effects, about the same number who quit the medications within a month; three-quarters stop taking antidepressants within six months. Although side effects can be problematic, the typical negative this isn't going to work anyway attitude also tends to undermine the patient's efforts. Many give up and don't have the persistence to switch medications and go through the trial and error that's sometimes required.

For those who decide the benefits outweigh the side effects and stay on an antidepressant, side effects are seldom problematic. In fact, after two years, about 85 percent of people taking an antidepressant report no problematic side effects.

When compared with the older antidepressants, the SSRIs cause less dry mouth, constipation, sedation, and weight gain, which bode well for long-term treatment. One of the primary reasons for quitting SSRIs, though, is a sexual problem (low libido, difficulty reaching orgasm).

It's one thing to have a sexual problem for a few weeks; it's quite another if the problem persists for months. Usually sexual difficulties can be dealt with by reducing the SSRI dose, changing antidepressants, or using certain medications as an antidote (such as Viagra). Bupropion (Wellbutrin XL), nefazodone (Serzone), and mirtazapine (Remeron) have the best sexual side effect profiles of all the newer antidepressants.

Other common problems associated with SSRIs are mild and usually temporary, and vary widely from person to person. These include gastrointestinal problems (i.e., diarrhea or upset stomach), insomnia or sleepiness, nervousness, sweating, tremors, and dizziness.

Most Common Side Effects of SSRIs and Tricyclics		
Side Effects	**Keep in Mind**	**Treatment Approach**
Nausea, diarrhea, gastrointestinal problems	Tend to fade over time	Take stool softeners, eat a high fiber diet, take just after eating
Agitation, mild tremor, and impulsivity	A particular problem for those with anxiety or insomnia	Reduce dose, add an antianxiety medication
Dry mouth	May boost risk for cavities and mouth sores	Drink plenty of water, suck on sugarless hard candy, use a saliva substitute, chew gum, take vitamin C tablets, rinse mouth frequently
Insomnia		

(*continues*)

Most Common Side Effects of SSRIs and Tricyclics (*continued*)		
Side Effects	Keep in Mind	Treatment Approach
Drowsiness		Take medication at night
Fatigue, weakness		
Dizziness		
Headache		
Sexual dysfunction	Delayed or no orgasm	Weekend breaks from medication can help; switch to a different atypical antidepressant or add sildenafil (Viagra) or a related medication

It's important to stay on the medication and talk to your doctor about side effects. Again, don't let habitual pessimism ruin your chances for successful treatment.

IF MEDICATION HELPS

If medication helps, your doctor will probably recommend that you stay on it for at least six to nine months. Then, depending on your circumstances and stressors, your doctor can help you decide whether to gradually discontinue it (over four to eight weeks) or to stay on it.

If the medication helps but you decide to go off of it to see what happens or because you don't like its side effects, there's a 50 percent likelihood that you will become depressed again within six months. Within four years, there's almost a 90 percent chance of a relapse. On the other hand, if you stay on medication, you are likely to continue to improve over time and it will be very unlikely that you will have a relapse. The most common cause of relapse among people taking antidepressants is nonadherence to the regimen.

More and more clinicians are advising, therefore, that if medication helps, a person with dysthymia should probably stay on it indefinitely. Dysthymia is a chronic condition—like diabetes—and can be very difficult to treat. Unless you have been in psychotherapy, the risk of becoming depressed again is very high and puts you at risk for a multitude of problems. We don't know yet if the self-help skills discussed in chapter 5 can actually reduce the risk of relapse. There is also some indication, though the final word is far from in, that going on and off medication may make you about 10 percent less likely to respond as well next time to the medication, presumably because of the way that recurring episodes of depression alter brain function and structure. That's another reason why many clinicians encourage people with dysthymia to stay on medication indefinitely.

If you find a medication that helps but you don't like the side effects, consider the benefits vs. side effects.

The known risks of dysthymia are usually far greater than the side effects of the newer antidepressants. Side effects are rarely harmful and usually can be remedied by decreasing dosage or switching medications.

However, sexual dysfunction and weight gain are the primary reasons why many people quit antidepressants. Tell your doctor if a side effect is making you think about stopping your medication.

If the medication is helping, don't worry that the effects will fade. The benefits tend to persist for as long as you take the medication. Even if you are in psychotherapy, the biochemical imbalances that the medication has helped to normalize are likely to reoccur if medication is stopped.

If you want to quit the medication because of side effects, consider how you assumed that the way you viewed the world was an entrenched personality trait. When the right medication works, you can feel completely normal and alive again! So talk to your doctor about options.

The Selective Serotonin Reuptake Inhibitors (SSRIs)

The first choices for dysthymia are the SSRIs, which include fluoxetine (Prozac), paroxetine (Paxil), sertraline (Zoloft), citalopram (Celexa), and escitalopram (Lexapro), because of their safety and tolerability. These medications are preferred because they are proven to work, relatively easy to prescribe, and generally well tolerated.

Put simply, these medications appear to enhance the availability of the biochemical serotonin in the brain. Serotonin affects many functions in the body, including sleep, appetite, libido, and the regulation of some hormones. Low brain levels of serotonin are linked to chronic stress, impulsivity, and moodiness. In animal studies, the loss of social dominance is associated with a decline in serotonin levels.

Restoring serotonin's imbalances not only helps brighten mood and restore normal sleeping and eating patterns, but it also seems to promote a sense of well-being.

> "Most dramatically, raising the level of serotonin seems to enhance security, courage, assertiveness, self-worth, calm, flexibility, resilience. Serotonin sets the tone . . . a feeling of security goes a long way . . . many things will go right when an animal, including a human animal, feels safe."
>
> —Peter Kramer, *Listening to Prozac*

More details about these medications that target serotonin in the brain are spelled out in the chart in Appendix 2; here are some highlights:

How SSRIs Compare		
Brand name	**Generic name**	**What you should know**
Prozac	fluoxetine	The most widely studied SSRI, now available as a generic (i.e., less expensive) drug. More insomnia and anxiety than others. Available as weekly tablet
Paxil	paroxetine	Best studied SSRI for anxiety, withdrawal more of a problem. Available as a generic
Zoloft	sertraline	Best studied SSRI for dysthymia, more diarrhea than with the other SSRIs.
Celexa	citalopram	Has few interactions with other medications, so a good choice for the elderly. Available as a generic
Luvox	fluvoxamine	Widely used in Europe and Japan but only approved in U.S. for treatment of obsessive compulsive disorder. May be more sedating but may cause less sexual dysfunction than the more widely used SSRIs
Lexapro	escitalopram	Very similar to Celexa but more potent

Other Newer Antidepressants

While serotonin is strongly connected to mood and depression, nore-pinephrine (also called noradrenaline), another brain chemical, is linked to depression but also more to motivation, energy level, productivity, and ability to concentrate as well as to the sleeping cycle and digestive and endocrine functions. Some newer antidepressants target or balance norepinephrine, either in combination with serotonin or another brain chemical, dopamine, and don't fit well into other antidepressant categories, so they're often called atypical antidepressants. None are approved for children under age 18.

Sometimes these medications are better tolerated than some SSRIs and almost always better tolerated than tricyclic medications, though they may cause some dizziness and dry mouth. The long-term side effects of these newer medications, however, are not as well studied as the other classes of antidepressants.

Details about these medications that target serotonin in the brain are spelled out in the chart in Appendix 2; here are some highlights:

How Atypical Antidepressants Compare		
Brand name	**Generic name**	**What you should know**
Wellbutrin	bupropion	Causes few sexual problems, can promote weight loss, also used to help quit smoking (Zyban). Also available as a generic
Effexor	venlafaxine	Evidence of stronger antidepressant effects, side effects profile like an SSRI, but can raise blood pressure
Cymbalta	duloxetine	Evidence of stronger antidepressant effects, side effect profile similar to venlafaxine, though it may not cause elevated blood pressure nearly as often
Serzone	nefazodone	Fewer sexual side effects and helps sleep but rarely used due to rare but serious liver damage
Desyrel	trazodone	Helps relieve insomnia
Remeron	mirtazapine	Works more quickly than most antidepressants, helps relieve anxiety and insomnia

The Tricyclic Antidepressants (TCAs)

These medications have been around a long time and often require more dose adjustments than the newer medications. They were the first-line approach to depression for years because they too enhanced norepinephrine and (for several) serotonin in depression. Although at least as effective as the SSRIs, side effects are fairly common and include weight gain, dry mouth, difficulty urinating, fatigue and drowsiness, constipation, blurred vision, sexual dysfunction, and dizziness upon standing suddenly. Because of the side effects, many people give up on these drugs before they've had a chance to kick in. Another drawback of the TCAs is that they can be lethal in overdose. For these reasons, a newer antidepressant is typically used before a TCA.

But when several SSRIs aren't effective, trying a TCA still may make good sense. A TCA still will help 30 to 50 percent of the time. Some distinctions of the TCAs are that

- All are available in generic form (i.e., less expensive)
- Uncommon side effects can be serious, affecting heart rhythm and causing fainting spells
- Some research suggests that men and older women respond better to the TCAs than younger women.

Monoamine Oxidase Inhibitors (MAOIs)

When a number of the widely used drugs don't work, therapy with a MAOI may be worth a try. Several studies have shown MAOIs to be effective for dysthymia. There are three MAOIs available in the U.S.: phenelzine (Nardil), tranycypromine (Parnate), and isocarboxazid (Marplan). These medications are thought to work by blocking an enzyme called monoamine oxidase, which degrades or destroys serotonin, norepinephrine, and dopamine.

Unfortunately, monoamine oxidase also plays an important role in the digestive system, where it breaks down natural chemicals that can elevate blood pressure. The most notorious is tyramine, which is found in certain foods and with an MAOI, can cause a severe hypertension reaction, which can be a life-threatening problem. People who take these drugs must avoid foods with a high tyramine content (some common ones are yogurt, pickles, aged cheeses, dried meat, sauerkraut, vermouth, chicken livers, canned figs, fava beans, red wine, and beer).

Other side effects include drowsiness, insomnia, dizziness, weight gain, and sexual dysfunction.

When taking a MAOI, you also need to avoid drug interactions with many other medications. Check with your physician before taking any other medications, including common over-the-counter cough medications and decongestants.

Combining Medications

Sometimes it's necessary to take two medications at once for treatment of dysthymia. Since it's very time consuming to wait the several months to see if an antidepressant is working, your doctor may suggest adding a second medication rather than simply switching. If one antidepressant is helping but only partially, rather than have you spend weeks transitioning to a different antidepressant, your doctor might try to strengthen the effects of a medication by adding another from a different class. Or, in a different situation, your physician might suggest a second antidepressant to relieve the side effects of the first medication.

Some commonly prescribed combinations are to:

- Enhance antidepressant effects by supplementing an SSRI or SNRI with bupropion (Wellbutrin)
- Improve sexual dysfunction caused by the antidepressant by adding bupropion or buspirone (Buspar)
- Address anxiety by combining an SSRI with buspirone (BuSpar) or a benzodiazepine, such as clonazepam or lorazepam
- Address insomnia (by combining an SSRI with mirtazapine [Remeron])

THYROID SUPPLEMENTS

Low levels of thyroid hormone (hypothyroidism) are common in women and sometimes unrecognized in dysthymia. Antidepressants probably do not work well if thyroid function is low. Thyroid supplementation has shown good results for dysthymia, and sometimes it's useful in addition to antidepressant medication. Several studies have reported that thyroid hormone combined with an antidepressant had very mild side effects and was very effective in half of the patients who had not responded to antidepressants. Preliminary studies with fairly high doses of thyroxine (T4) have been promising (showing improvement in about half the cases of treatment-resistant patients with chronic depression and/or dysthymia), even with some people who had fairly normal thyroid levels.

If thyroid supplementation is suggested, it's important that you get your thyroid levels checked by a physician and consult with him or her about which thyroid supplements to take.

ESTROGEN

Estrogen replacement therapy (ERT) may relieve menopausal- and perimenopausal-associated depression and even relieve depression in older women who do not respond to standard antidepressants. ERT has other health benefits and risks that you should discuss with your physician. (Hormone replacement therapy that contains both progesterone and estrogen may even cause mild depression.)

Estrogen, which is available in patches or pills, may be a good choice for perimenopausal or menopausal women with mild depression who have no history of depression. Estrogen may also be used to supplement antidepressant therapy especially in older women who are experiencing menopause.

Of course, any hormone supplementation must be prescribed and monitored by a physician. For more details about estrogen therapy and depression, see chapter 12 on hormones.

On the Front Line

Current research focuses on learning more about the types of depression and whether those resulting from genetic vs. psychosocial causes respond differently to therapies. New research is also looking into new medications that may target one type of depression over another, have fewer side effects, and work more quickly. With more than 15 serotonin receptors, and only a few of them linked to antidepressive effects, researchers are looking into increasingly specific medications. Here are a few of tomorrow's hopefuls.

Reboxetine (Edronax) is a selective noradrenaline reuptake inhibitor that's not available in the United States. Reboxetine has been well studied in Europe and has been shown to be effective for depression.

Amisulpride (an atypical antipsychotic, which in a low dose acts as a dopamine enhancer) is an antipsychotic drug used in Europe to treat schizophrenia. Several studies show that low-dose therapy amisulpride can significantly relieve the symptoms of dysthymia.

Moclobemide (Aurorix, Manerix), a newer MAOI, which is available in Europe, is much better tolerated (even better than tricyclics) than the older MAOIs and has been shown to be effective for dysthymia. In a 2000 study, 2 percent of patients taking moclobemide reported sexual problems vs. 22 percent of those taking SSRIs. It is not yet available in the United States.

Seligiline (Emsamtop). This drug is also a selective MAOI and is currently approved in pill form as a low-dose therapy for Parkinson's disease. The drug delivered via a skin patch permits high doses of seligiline to be used without dietary restrictions.

Tianeptine (and amineptine). The new drug tianeptine (Stablon), is chemically related to amineptine (Survector), which is no longer available. Amineptine was a drug unique in that it was a dopamine reuptake inhibitor. While tianeptine is chemically related to amineptine, it is not a dopamine reuptake inhibitor. Instead, it has a totally unique action: it appears to work exactly opposite to the SSRIs by enhnacing serotonin reuptake.

8

◆ ◆ ◆

Exercise and Nutrition

Reading is to the mind what
exercise is to the body.

—Sir Richard Steele

There is little doubt that certain lifestyle changes can go a long way to promote good mental health. The effects of exercise in particular are well researched (probably because it's easier to study than nutrition), and a growing body of evidence confirms the powerful influence of exercise on buoying mood and helping dysthymia and mild depression.

Exercise: Good for Your Body and Good for Your Mind

For dysthymia and other forms of mild and moderate depression, several studies have found that exercise is as powerful an antidepressant as psychotherapy or medication. Moderate, regular exercise can significantly lift mood and self-esteem, and improve sleep patterns, one's sense of mastery, and the ability to cope with stress. In fact, exercise seems to significantly influence almost all the symptoms of dysthymia.

Just do it, as the Nike ad urges: exercise benefits both the body and the mind.

A 1999 review paper that examined dozens of studies from three decades of research concluded that exercise never fails to work, either as the primary or a supplemental treatment for mild to moderate depression. Just as effective as cognitive-behavioral group therapy, five weeks of moderate exercise, twice a week (even a walk) was enough to do the trick. Other studies, such as a study of 156 mildly and moderately depressed volunteers conducted at Duke University Medical Center, found that volunteers fared as well on exercise as those on an SSRI medication (Zoloft or sertraline), and the effect was still significant four months later.

The benefits of exercise are that it

- Is inexpensive
- Works promptly in 10 days (30 minutes per day)—even just walking
- Works when other therapies are refused
- Is versatile: any type works—aerobic, strength training, or weight bearing

The effects of an exercise program are so beneficial that it should always be part of someone's course of therapy, and it's rather shocking when it's not. Exercise is so effective that the American Psychological Association has issued an official statement endorsing its importance and promoting this vastly underused treatment for mild to moderate depression.

Ideally, you should exercise four to six times a week for at least 20 minutes during which the heart rate increases to a sustained level determined by your age.

You may not be able to control a lot of things, but you can control when and how you exercise.

HOW EXERCISE HELPS

How Exercise Works	
Boosts certain brain chemicals	By influencing availability of endorphins, adrenaline, serotonin, and dopamine in the brain which contribute to a sense of well-being; may also boost levels of phenylethylamine (PEA), a chemical related to the runner's high
Promotes physical health	By promoting weight loss, improving flexibility and muscle tone, reducing risk of obesity, heart disease, cancer, high blood pressure, osteoporosis, diabetes
	(continues)

How Exercise Works (*continued*)	
Relieves tension, frustration and anger, stress, and anxiety	By changing heart rate and oxygen intake, stimulating biochemical changes.
Increases social contacts	By providing social interactions around the exercise activities
Promotes a sense of mastery and boosts self-esteem	Just by doing it, you feel a sense of accomplishment
Decreases rumination and self-destructive thoughts	By distracting your attention
Improves sleep quality	By stimulating muscles, lungs, heart rate, oxygen intake, and biochemical changes
Relieves guilt and boosts pleasure	By allowing you to eat more freely without guilt; that freedom to enjoy food is a deep pleasure and satisfaction

It is the very symptoms of dysthymia that may discourage you from exercising—fatigue, little energy, passivity, feelings of helplessness and hopelessness. If you don't want to exercise, try the follow approaches.

- Force yourself to do something: start with easy stretching and strolling on a regular basis
- Build up gradually to walking and fast walking
- Do what you enjoy—choose a form of exercise you like
- Find someone to do it with

If in therapy, consider walking with the therapist—some therapists welcome this.

Diet and Nutrition

Studying the effects of diet on dysthymia is much more complex than studying the effects of exercise. We do know, however, that a good diet can help to combat depression by providing plenty of energy, a stable blood sugar level, and adequate nutrients for the production of neurotransmitters and other vital substances. A good diet consists of plenty of fresh vegetables, fresh fruits, and whole grain breads and cereals, plenty of fiber, the B complex vitamins, iron, proteins and the recommended dietary allowances of other vitamins and minerals.

If your diet might not be providing what you should have, take a daily multivitamin to ensure adequate levels of critical nutrients that can contribute to depression. There is no evidence that specific vitamin supplements have strong antidepressant effects.

CAFFEINE AND SUGAR

Many of the studies on caffeine seem to contradict each other: on the one hand, some suggest caffeine is a mild antidepressant as consumption of caffeinated beverages is linked to a lower incidence of suicide. On the other hand, caffeine (and sugar) is thought to worsen mood swings, and caffeine addiction may contribute to depression, according to some researchers. The bottom line is that caffeine may initially make you more alert for an hour or so but then more sluggish as you come down from the boost. To see how caffeine affects you, decrease your intake by at least 50 percent for a week and see if you feel better or worse.

Sugar may trigger a similar effect. You initially may feel a surge of energy, a sugar rush, but an hour later as your blood sugar plummets, you are sapped of energy, which may make you feel less confident and less sure of yourself. When this condition of low blood sugar is chronic, it is diagnosed as hypoglycemia, that is, abnormal carbohydrate (sugar) metabolism. It can deprive the brain of some the glucose (sugar) it needs and may lead to a host of symptoms, including depression and fatigue. Several studies from the University of Philadelphia, for example, suggest that people who are depressed have trouble controlling their blood sugar (either through abnormal glucose control or insulin resistance), so these researchers recommend low sugar, low carbohydrate diets. By the same token, depression can contribute to poor blood sugar control indirectly, by its classic symptoms of passivity and apathy, which would lead to a lack of physical exercise, a gain in weight, and perhaps a poorer diet with more junk food.

A lot of people use a combination of caffeine and sugar to stay energized, having a caffeinated drink or a high-sugar treat every few hours. These so-called comfort foods can leave you not only vulnerable to mood swings every few hours but also susceptible to a cycle of dependence that promotes poor nutrition and weight gain, which, in turn, could make you more prone to feeling down on yourself.

VITAMINS AND OTHER NUTRITIONAL SUPPLEMENTS

For dysthymia, research regarding supplements is scant. Various recommendations include folic acid, tyrosine, iron, vitamin B3 or niacin (which is involved in the production of tryptophan), vitamin B6 (especially in women taking birth control pills or who experience premenstrual syndrome), folate, and vitamin B1. These recommendations are based on perhaps an isolated small study here or there, folklore, or anecdotal success stories.

Vitamin B Complex. Some researchers report that people who are depressed tend to have low levels of the B vitamins (including B6, B12, and folic acid) in their bodies and some recommend supplements of particular nutrients. Whether to take a B complex supplement is somewhat controversial: some nutritionists recommend such supplements while others think they're unnecessary and a bad idea. The safest bet would be to ensure that your multivitamin includes plenty of these B vitamins.

Folate (vitamin B folate or folic acid) may enhance the effectiveness of SSRIs and other antidepressants. According to several studies, up to 35 percent of depressed persons and up to 90 percent of elderly depressed persons are folate deficient. Thus, some practitioners recommend between 400 and 800 mcg a day, especially for women and for those who don't respond initially to antidepressant treatment, to treat depression. Others suggest that any multivitamin supplement include folate.

Iron. Low iron levels are clearly linked to fatigue and low energy, and thus, could contribute to depressive feelings. If you feel listless and have little energy, consider getting your iron levels checked. Iron supplements are widely available and are often recommended for women in their childbearing years (because of monthly blood loss through menstruation).

Amino acids. Several amino acids or amino acid derivatives, including phenylalanine, tyrosine, acetyl-L-carnitine, and phosphatidylserine have been linked to depression in small preliminary studies. The thinking is that specific amino acids are required for the synthesis of neurotransmitters.

Tryptophan is an amino acid that plays a role in the production of serotonin. Some research suggests that tryptophan deficiencies can make the symptoms of a major depression worse, whereas a rich trytophan diet may help enhance the effects of prescribed antidepressants. Foods high in tryptophan include high carbohydrate, high protein foods, such as soy products, seafood, meat, whole grains, beans, and rice. Tryptophan supplements have been removed from the market after some were found to be contaminated and linked to serious problems.

One by-product of tryptophan is a substance called 5-hydroxytryptophan or 5-htp, which has been claimed to help boost serotonin production. Some people take it as a supplement for depression but considering that it is a hormone precursor, any supplement with 5-htp should be cleared by a physician.

Vitamin D. Vitamin D has also been suggested as having an impact on psychological functioning and in small preliminary studies has been associated with improved moods.

Omega-3 fatty acids. Omega-3 polyunsaturated fatty acids, which are found in cold-water fish (such as tuna or salmon), may be beneficial for depression. Omega-3 fatty acids are critical to the synthesis of cell membranes and hence are relevant to neuron activity. Some researchers point out that Americans are eating fewer foods that are high in omega-3 fatty acids, and as a result, levels of several of their derivatives (especially eicosapentaenoic acid [EPA] and docosahexaenoic acid [DHA]) are lower in the body. DHA, which is not only in cold-water fish but also in eggs, organ meats, and red meats. When used as a supplement for depression, omega-3 fatty acids may boost the effects of antidepressants.

If other studies currently under way confirm this link, omega-3 fatty acids may be considered a type of nontoxic mood stabilizer with antidepressant effects, though it's still too soon to know.

NADH. Various other nutrients have been associated with depression in a small study here or there, such as NADH (nicotinamide adenine dinucleotide), a coenzyme involved in the production of adenosine triphosphate (ATP), the body's main source of intracellular energy, and perhaps with the synthesis of the neurotransmitter norepinephrine, magnesium, and vitamin C among other compounds found in the body.

To ensure that you are not deficient in any of these nutrients, a high-quality multivitamin may make sense; make sure it has folate and the RDA (recommended dietary allowance as set by the federal government) for iron. However, any supplementation of individual nutrients, particularly in megadoses above the RDA, should be checked out with a physician, especially if you are on any medications.

9

◆ ◆ ◆

Herbal and Other Types
of Supplements

St. John's wort and other supplements have been touted for years as "natural" approaches to treating depression. Although few have proven useful for major depression—which is a serious illness that must be vigorously treated—a few have intriguing possibilities for milder depressions and, possibly, dysthymia. One problem with herbal therapies is that no major pharmaceutical company will devote the millions of dollars it takes to test if an herbal therapy works, is safe, and to bring it to market. Because these supplements are already widely available, don't require a prescription, and cost less than prescribed antidepressants, companies have no profit motive to pursue them, whether or not they have a therapeutic effect.

Another problem is that just because a supplement is "natural"—that is, derived from herbs or hormones that the body produces anyway—doesn't mean it is safer than a synthetic drug. Supplements have not been stringently tested and so are not regulated or standardized the way that Food and Drug Administration (FDA)-approved products are. As a result, you sometimes don't know how much of the desired ingredient is actually in the supplement or how much might most benefit you; you also might not know as much about a supplement's purity, effectiveness, or safety—or dangers—as you do about FDA-approved products. These are biochemically active compounds and a physician should clear any use of them.

St. John's Wort

The herbal supplement St. John's wort (*Hypericum perforatum*) has been used for years to treat depression. Tremendously popular in Germany where it's the leading type of antidepressant prescribed, St. John's wort (SJW) is widely available in the United States in capsule, tea, ointment, and tincture form. In 1998, it was one of the top ten herbal supplements sold, accounting for some $400 million in sales.

But, does it work?

A recent study that looked at eight brands of St. John's wort found that only two contained enough active ingredient (hypericin) to be therapeutic.

HOW EFFECTIVE IS ST. JOHN'S WORT?

More than two dozen European studies have looked at SJW and its effectiveness in treating depression, and many of these studies included mild depression, such as dysthymia. It appears that SJW must be taken at a dose of 900 to 1,200 milligrams of hypericin each day to be effective. A 1996 review of most of these studies (which included 20 double-blind trials—the gold standard of experimental studies), assessing a total of 1,757 people with mild to moderate depression and published in the prestigious *British Medical Journal*, concluded that for these milder depressions SJW *is* not only more effective than a placebo but just as effective as antidepressant medication but with fewer side effects. Specifically, the researchers found:

SJW	Prescription Antidepressants
64% felt significantly better	59% felt significantly better
4% dropped out due to side effects	8% dropped out due to side effects

However, critics point out that many of these studies were flawed in that:

- Many were small and short-term (none went beyond eight weeks)
- Many studies did not use standard doses for SJW

- None looked at long-term effects
- Most used different diagnostic criteria than Americans do
- Many lacked a control group (although some were double-blind studies and had a control group)
- Many used self-reports of depression and improvements rather than professional assessments

In 2001, the first large-scale, multicenter, randomized, placebo-controlled study of SJW was published in one of the most authoritative journals: the *Journal of the American Medical Association*. In comparing how 200 people with major depression fared with either SJW or a placebo, the researchers found the herb to be no more effective than the placebo. However, the researchers did not evaluate the herb's effects on mild or moderate depression.

The results of a major multicenter study funded by the National Institutes of Health's National Center for Complementary and Alternative Medicine, Office of Dietary Supplements failed to shed more light on just how effective SJW is for major depressions. The study compared SJW, a placebo, and the SSRI Zoloft (sertraline). Overall, neither SJW nor sertraline were significantly more effective than the placebo. This is what is called a "failed study"; when an antidepressant with known therapeutic activity fails to work, one cannot interpret the study as a negative against the novel compound.

Results of a third study were recently reported. In a European multicenter trial, SJW had significant antidepressant effects. What's going on here? Is it possible that SJW works in Europe and not in the United States? This seems unlikely. Rather, it appears that SJW has relatively weak or inconsistent effects that are not always apparent in every study. It also might be possible that SJW works better for some types of depression (perhaps including dysthymia) than for others.

For the time being, the bottom line is that without more good quality studies on SJW's benefits for dysthymia or other types of mild depression, conclusions regarding SJW's effects can't be drawn. However, many experts, including officials from the Agency for Health Care Policy and Research and the American College of Physicians-American Society of Internal Medicine, state that SJW appears to be more effective than a placebo for the short-term outpatient treatment of milder depressive disorders.

Thus, it might be worth a personal "empirical" trial, especially if you are not interested in seeking other treatment, are fully aware of the potential side effects, and receive your physician's okay.

SIDE EFFECTS

It is always a good idea to check with your doctor or pharmacist about any herbal products you plan to take on a regular basis. The reported side effects of SJW seem minor, but for some people they may be serious. Most people find SJW easy to tolerate, though some report dizziness, dry mouth, nausea, fatigue, and stomach upset. Rarely, people will experience skin sensitivity to light and will sunburn easily. The side effects are generally so mild or infrequent that only 1 to 4 percent of people stop taking SJW because of its obvious side effects (virtually identical to a placebo).

Recent studies, however, report that SJW can significantly interfere with the effectiveness of many medications: SJW can cause an increase in the activity of the liver enzymes that deactivate some medications.

A 2000 FDA public health advisory warned that SJW may trigger interactions with certain drugs. The following chart shows the particular classes of drugs and their generic and brand names that are of concern.

St. John's Wort and Interactions with Other Medications	
Drugs of concern	**Specific medicines identified as being affected by SJW**
Certain antibiotics	tetracycline antibiotics
Birth control pills	
Cholesterol-lowering drugs	Mevacor (lovastatin), Zocor (simvastatin), Procardia (nifedipine); Versed (midazolam), digoxin, theophylline, and possibly others
Statin drugs	
Cancer medications	
Seizure drugs	
Beta blockers	
Blood thinners	Coumadin (warfarin)
Calcium channel blockers	
Protease inhibitors for HIV infection	Crixivan (indinavir) and others
Immune suppressants	cyclosporine to prevent rejection of organ transplants

In addition, a recent report from Fordham University warns that SJW not only may make you more vulnerable to the effects of bright light (i.e., sunburn) but also seems linked to a higher rate of cataracts. The researchers recommend wearing sunglasses if you take SJW and they discourage the use of tanning beds. It also would seem to be unwise to use light therapy for winter depression when taking SJW.

HOW ST. JOHN'S WORT WORKS

Although extracts of SJW include a host of chemical components, the active ingredients are thought to be hyperforin and hypericin. This is why some companies now are standardizing their dose of hypericin and hyperforin.

Research suggests that SJW may have antidepressant effects by helping to keep certain neurotransmitters—especially serotonin but also perhaps noradrenaline and dopamine—available to the brain. However, this is not because of inhibition of serotonin reuptake (the way SSRIs, selective serotonin reuptake inhibitors, work), nor is it because of the inhibition of monoamine oxidase. Evidently, the hypericin in SJW reduces levels of a stress-related protein called interleukin-6 (IL-6). Raised levels of IL-6 are associated with depression. Other possibly active ingredients may include polycyclic phenols and pseudohypericin.

RECOMMENDATIONS

SJW is generally a safe supplement, but it is not necessarily harmless nor is it inert. There's little doubt that it has biological effects, and when considering a course of SJW, you need to weigh the costs vs. the benefits, watch for side effects, and consider giving the supplement four to six weeks before you see results. Since more than half of all those with depressive disorders don't seek any treatment, taking SJW may be worth a concerted try.

If you take St. John's wort:

- Consider SJW an experimental treatment. Give it 6 to 8 weeks to work and, if it doesn't, move on to another form of therapy.
- Look for a reputable brand, a hypericin concentration of 0.3 percent, and a label with the words "standardized extract."
- Take 900 mg a day: 300 mg three times a day for at least four weeks.
- Tell your doctor you take SJW. A study at the Mayo Clinic found that 60 percent of those who take herbal supplements do not mention it to their doctors. *This can be dangerous*.

- Stop taking SJW if you start taking a prescribed antidepressant.
- Stop taking SJW if you are prescribed any of the medications listed on page 121; better yet, ask your doctor about SJW if you take *any* prescription medications.
- Stop taking SJW at least two to three weeks before any surgery.
- SJW is not appropriate for children or pregnant or nursing women.
- *Beware of sun exposure. You may burn faster when taking St. John's wort. Wear a hat in the sun and wraparound sunglasses. Be particularly careful at the beach or skiing. Do not combine SJW and light therapy, and avoid tanning beds.*

Other Herbal Remedies

Health food stores, websites, and alternative health publications offer a host of other supplements that might influence dysthymia and depression. Many of these recommendations stem from a small published study here or there that sometimes didn't even use a dose available on the open market. But the findings from such preliminary studies get into the folklore of natural remedies and sometimes are promoted widely.

Research is very scant on the following products and caution should be used in trying them. Remember: Just because they are "natural" does not necessarily mean they are safe. Some have caused very serious, even lethal side effects. Also keep in mind that these products aren't regulated and have poorer quality control. On the other hand, just because products haven't been well studied doesn't mean that some are not potentially very helpful. One of these supplements, S-adenosylmethionine (SAM-e, for short), in particular, needs to be looked at in more detail as it has garnered an extraordinary amount of publicity.

SAM-E (PRONOUNCED "SAMMY")

In 1999, SAM-e hit the U.S. marketplace. SAM-e is short for S-adenosylmethionine, a substance that is present in all our cells and plays a vital role in at least 35 biological functions and biochemical reactions, such as keeping cell membranes elastic, contributing to the production of brain neurotransmitters (including the critical ones related to depression: serotonin, norepinephrine, and dopamine), helping in the transmission of nerve impulses, and promoting joint repair (that's why it's prescribed for arthritis). But it also may influence emotions and moods, among other important interactions.

Available in Europe for more than 20 years as a prescription medication to treat depression and arthritis, SAM-e debuted in the United States with a best-selling book about it by a reputable author: *Stop Depression Now: SAM-e, The Breakthrough Supplement That Works as Well as Prescription Drugs in Half the Time . . . with No Side Effects* by psychopharmacologist Richard P. Brown, M.D., an associate professor of clinical psychiatry at Columbia University College of Physicians and Surgeons.

Overnight, SAM-e became a dietary supplement sensation when major media such as *Time*, *Newsweek*, and ABC News, quoted Brown about SAM-e's effectiveness for depression.

SAM-e is a methyl donor—that is, a compound that carries and gives methyl groups to other molecules, such as cell membrane components and neurotransmitters; methyl donors play important roles in energy metabolism, immune function, and nerve function. Thus, SAM-e is not an herb, hormone, vitamin, or nutrient but a synthetic form of the chemical produced in the body that's been stabilized for a longer shelf life.

More than 40 clinical trials—most in Europe and a few recent ones in the United States—have been conducted. Some have linked low blood levels of SAM-e to depression; others have found SAM-e effective for depression. But none of them has been truly decisive. Nevertheless, some researchers believe SAM-e might be beneficial; in fact, a Harvard Medical School team believed in it enough to undertake at SAM-e study in 2002 to see how effective it is in combination with a prescription antidepressant. The jury's still out.

Chemically, SAM-e is totally unrelated to the conventional antidepressants. As with SJW, SAM-e may be worth a try for dysthymia if conventional treatments are not of interest. Unlike SJW, however, SAM-e is expensive, and it's not covered by medical insurance.

SAM-e has certain advantages:

- No prescription is needed
- Side effects are relatively few and mild (loose bowel movements and headache are occasionally reported)
- Sexual function is not affected, unlike many depression medications
- It appears safe (though no one knows for sure)
- It works quickly (people report changes within a week, compared to four to six weeks for tricyclic antidepressants and SSRIs)

Brown, a specialist in depressions that don't respond to conventional approaches, says he got involved with SAM-e after his patients who swore by it for depression and arthritis convinced him to do so.

For dysthymia and other forms of mild depression, Brown recommends 400 mg a day. (He recommends higher doses for major depression when other antidepressants don't work but only under the supervision of a professional.) A well-informed expert on mild and major depression, Brown also stresses exercise, relaxation techniques (yoga and meditation), healthful eating habits, and cognitive techniques to reduce obsessive, destructive thought patterns.

Warning

People with a major depression should be under a doctor's care. Remedies like SAM-e or SJW should not be tried when the depression is incapacitating or associated with psychotic features (hallucinations or delusions) or prior mood swings (manic depression). Nor should prescribed antidepressants be stopped suddenly (to switch to SAM-e) without a doctor's supervision.

In addition to its cost and risk, SAM-e has encountered problems of standardization and fraud. SAM-e is difficult to produce because the active ingredient is unstable. You have no guarantee that the pills you buy have been properly handled. A *Consumer Reports* magazine study (December 2000) tested 12 brands of SAM-e. Eight brands had more SAM-e than their labels claimed and 4 brands had less. Only 6 of the 12 brands were enteric coated, an important factor to ensure proper absorption. A *Good Housekeeping* lab tested 8 brands of SAM-e and found that 5 had more SAM-e than the label claimed and 2 had less. One brand had no SAM-e at all! Brown's lab tested 8 major brands of SAM-e and found that 2 contained no SAM-e.

SAM-e has not been studied to compare its effectiveness against the SSRI antidepressants. It has also not been studied for treating obsessive compulsive disorder or other anxiety disorders.

One of the biggest problems with SAM-e is that it is converted into homocysteine in the body. High levels of homocysteine increase the risk of heart disease. SAM-e is likely to promote higher levels, though no one knows how high. Further, a 2000 *Consumer Reports* study reports that the cost of a daily dose of 400 mg of SAM-e ranges from $1.80 to $8.75. This is no less expensive than a name brand antidepressant and, often, much more so.

If you take SAM-e:

- Tell your doctor about your supplements.
- Be sure any SAM-e pills you buy are foil wrapped, enteric-coated, and contain 1,4-butanedislfonate, a stabilizer.
- To maintain SAM-e's stability, don't take it out of its foil blister pack until you are ready to take it. If left out, SAM-e will lose its effectiveness.
- Keep your diet high in fruits and vegetables and take a multivitamin. As SAM-e boosts homocysteine levels, which increase the risk of heart disease, be sure you get plenty of the three B vitamins—folic acid, B6, and B-12—which can lower homocysteine levels.

Although a person is probably more likely to benefit from a traditional approach to relieve dysthymia—antidepressant medication or cognitive or interpersonal therapy—if for no other reason than that they've been widely tested, a course of SAM-e for someone who won't pursue the tested treatments appears to be safe. Ideally, if you take it, you are under the supervision of a professional.

INOSITOL

Inositol is a sugarlike substance that the body uses to produce healthy nerve cell membranes. It is therefore important for nerve transmission and other functions. Several preliminary studies have found inositol levels to be low in people who were depressed. Inositol supplementation also was found to be a safe and possibly effective treatment for depression. A dose of 12 grams a day of inositol is typically used. Before running off and starting inositol, however, keep in mind that the amount of evidence evaluating its antidepressant effects is less than one-five-hundredth of that for standard medications—meaning that prescription antidepressants have had 500 times more studies done about them than inositol.

DHEA (DEHYDROEPIANDROSTERONE)

DHEA, a hormone that is easily converted into estrogen and testosterone, is sold as a dietary supplement and has been touted to help promote weight loss, relieve depression, and improve energy. Several small preliminary studies have found that people with depression and dysthymia may have low levels of DHEA. Supplementation (90 to 300 mg a day of DHEA) may in fact help relieve dysthymia. However, DHEA is an adrenal steroid and, in large doses, it can have serious side effects; thus, it should not be taken without a doctor's approval.

MORE HERBS

With depression being so widespread, herbalists sometimes recommend a host of other natural remedies that have, perhaps, a small study or two to support them. Although we don't recommend any of these, as evidence is too scant to confirm that they are useful, individuals can judge for themselves whether they'd like to try some of them. Again, be sure to tell your doctor about any supplements you take on a regular basis.

Kava kava is a root that has been studied because of its antianxiety properties. Several European studies suggest that kava kava may be as effective for treating anxiety as standard medications. However, recent evidence indicates that kava kava can cause liver damage and sudden death in previously well people, and the U.S. Food and Drug Administration and Canadian and Australian officials have issued warnings regarding the root. Germany has banned its sale.

Valerian (Valerian officinalis) is often recommended for insomnia. Valerian may cause an adverse reaction with lorazepam (Ativan), and in some individuals, produces a feeling of "strangeness."

Damiana (Turnera diffusa) is sometimes recommended for sexual problems caused by antidepressant medication. Possible side effects include an adverse effect on blood sugar and a mild laxative effect; it is not recommended for persons with gastrointestinal or kidney disorders.

Ginseng is sometimes recommended to help cope with stress or anxiety. Possible side effects include headache, insomnia, anxiety, breast soreness or tenderness, skin rashes, asthma attacks, increased blood pressure, diarrhea, euphoria, nervousness, skin eruptions, heart palpitations, or postmenopausal uterine bleeding.

Ginkgo biloba is sometimes recommended for older people with memory problems. It also may be recommended for sexual problems due to antidepressant use. Possible side effects include headaches, seizures, irritability, restlessness, diarrhea, nausea, and vomiting.

Although herbal supplements might be useful therapies for dysthymia, their effectiveness and safety are not proven. There is not sufficient research to back up many of the claims made for them. And, although one needs no prescription for them, it's prudent to consult a doctor before self-medicating. These are active substances that are not necessarily harmless.

Next, we'll look at other strategies that seem to help some people.

10

◆ ◆ ◆

Supplemental Strategies

A journey of a thousand
miles begins with one step.

—Chinese Proverb

Life is a succession of moments,
to live each one is to succeed.

—Corita Kent, American artist

In addition to learning better coping strategies, combating negative styles of thinking, taking medication, exercising as often as possible, and perhaps taking herbal or nutritional supplements with your doctor's approval, you can help yourself in other ways as well.

These self-help strategies include

- Relaxation and stress management
- Seeking social support
- Sleep and light

Other strategies that involve treatment by professionals include biofeedback and acupuncture. An area for which there is little scientific research but appears to be safe is homeopathic remedies. Let's discuss these strategies in more detail.

Relaxation and Stress Management

For good mental health, it's important to know how to calm yourself down, especially since anxiety and depression are commonly associated conditions. Many studies have found that inducing the so-called relaxation response, a term coined by Herbert Bensen, M.D., can significantly reduce the activity of the fight-or-flight response of the autonomic nervous system under stress. These responses include racing heart, perspiration, dilated pupils, tightened muscles, and release of adrenaline and cortisol into the bloodstream. Although a stress response may be essential for survival in a life-and-death circumstance, prolonged stress responses adversely affect health in many ways.

Inducing the relaxation response—using techniques such as deep breathing, progressive muscle relaxation, meditation, guided imagery, visualization, massage, and yoga—can help reduce irritability, difficulty concentrating, and fatigue. Prerecorded tapes are available at bookstores to help to talk you through relaxation exercises.

By regularly practicing deep breathing exercises, for example, you learn how to progressively relax your muscles and slow your breathing, which in turn will help calm you down by reducing the release of stress hormones into your circulatory system.

A simple relaxation exercise

- Sit comfortably and close your eyes.
- Breathe in through your nose deeply and slowly, and push out your stomach (not your chest) to involve your diaphragm. Count to 3 slowly.
- On the exhale, out through your mouth, count to 6 slowly. After you get the rhythm, you can repeat a word or phrase in your mind instead of counting as you exhale slowly and completely.
- When your mind wanders, bring it back to listening to your breathing and continue to count.

Start with 5-minute exercises and try to increase to 20 minutes. Try to practice this exercise at least once a day.

Exercise for muscle relaxation

- In a darkened, private space, lie on the floor or a sofa with eyes shut and body comfortably relaxed. Repeat the same thought in 4 or 5 different ways. For example: "My arms are heavy and warm, very heavy and warm. My arms are getting even heavier and warmer. My arms are sinking, sinking down into the floor."

While repeating these statements, try to visualize a warm bath, bright sunshine, a cozy fireplace, or other things that bring warmth and pleasure. Repeat with every body part (substituting legs, neck, feet, back, and so on, in place of arms in the example) for as long as possible, breathing deeply and slowly. The objective is to put the mind and body into a relaxed, trancelike state.

Social Support and Social Contact

Studies show that regular contact with family members and friends with whom you have positive relationships can promote recovery from depression. People who have strong spiritual faiths—not necessarily organized religion—also are at lower risk of depression. An ideal way to pursue new social networks and connect to a sense of spirituality is to take a yoga, pilates, or meditation class, or go to services at a spiritual center. These activities not only are calming but may foster new ties that can expand your support network and present new opportunities for social and community service activities. In fact, many studies also show that volunteering and performing community service are powerful antidotes to dysthymia and depression.

Strengthening your support network

- List 5 people you can call on. Keep their phone numbers and e-mail addresses handy. Don't lean too heavily on any one for support.

- Join support groups
  a weight loss group
  a parenting group
  a single-parent group
  children and spouses of Alcoholics Anonymous

- Join special interest groups
  a book club
  a writer's circle
  a women's group
  a mother's group
  a religious/spiritual group

- Go to community events
  free concerts
  lectures
  library events
  local college events

- Help support others
  volunteer at a local service organization (Red Cross, literacy outreach, etc.)

- Keep in touch with friends and peers
  make a list of your primary and then your secondary circle of friends. Connect with the primary circle, and then with a few from the next circle. Phone or e-mail them.

- Develop appropriate social skills

Families and Friends Can Help

If you think or know that a loved one has dysthymia, here are some tips on how you can promote recovery.

Do

- Encourage the person to talk and assert himself
- Reassure the person that he has a right to express his anger and other negative feelings
- Encourage him to join groups, exercise, go out and seek help; offer to go with him
- Help reduce his isolation by talking with him, exercising with him, and going to social events with him.
- Remember: although you may be frustrated, he is miserable

Don't

- Blame the person for not snapping out of it; she has an illness
- Accuse her of being lazy or self-indulgent
- Tell her she has no reason to feel depressed
- Avoid her: she needs your support and companionship
- Tell her to pull herself together

Light Therapy

Exposure to bright light (light therapy or phototherapy) is widely accepted as an effective treatment for seasonal affective disorder (SAD or winter depression). It also is increasingly being considered for the treatment of nonseasonal depression, as well as of certain sleep disorders, bulimia, and depressions that occur with a woman's menstrual cycle (premenstrual dysphoric disorder). In fact, some experts consider light therapy as effective as antidepressant medications for seasonal depression, and there is some evidence that at times it may work for major or mild depression. Using light therapy with medication and psychotherapy for dysthymia may be synergistic—that is, the effect of them together is greater than just adding the effects of the two of them together; they enhance each other. It also works much quicker (a week vs. several months) and has far fewer side effects than medications.

Such a result makes sense if you consider how many different types of mammals experience changes in energy, appetite, and sexual interest as day length diminishes and they're exposed to less light.

Although plenty of bright sunshine could be adequate, most people can't get enough sunshine to make a difference for depression, especially on rainy days or in cold climates. The Cafe Engel, in Helsinki, Finland, for instance, advertises that it serves bright light with breakfast from October through March. Some standard values of light exposure, as measured by the lux (i.e., the light given off by one candle at a distance of one meter), are summarized below. Portable but powerful desktop light boxes (10,000 lux) can provide the adequate exposure if used 30 to 60 minutes each morning.

Let There Be Light: How Much Light Do You Get?	
Full moon, watching TV in dark	1 lux
Average evening living room	15 lux
Typical home	200–500 lux
A well-lit office	400–700 lux
Cloudy day or shade	2,500 lux
Sunny spring morning	10,000 lux
Typical light box	10,000 lux
High noon, spring on a sunny day	80,000 lux
Sunny day at the beach	100,000 lux

It's easiest to put the unit on a desk or in front of a TV or exercise bike. Daniel Kripke, M.D., a professor of psychiatry at the University of California, San Diego, recommends early morning light treatments for people who tend to sleep more than they should. If you nod off too early in the evening and then wake up too early the next morning, he suggests the light treatments in the evening.

As long as treatments don't exceed 10,000 lux, side effects are minimal, though some people initially experience eye strain, headache, irritability, or new sleep problems, in which case it'd be wise to turn down the intensity of the light or shorten the length of exposure.

Without a light box (which we don't recommend building on your own), it's virtually impossible to get the adequate brightness of light needed during the middle of the winter in many parts of the United States. Incandescent light can be diffused but it can be "hot" and is more expensive; fluorescent light is inexpensive and produces less heat but it doesn't have the full spectrum of natural light.

Light therapy alone may also be appropriate for the person not willing to take drugs or to engage in a series of therapy sessions, as well as pregnant women, young children, and people who have strong side effects to many different antidepressants.

Biofeedback

Biofeedback may help dysthymia by reducing stress, inducing calm, and improving sleep and concentration. It works by teaching you how to manipulate some physiological activities that used to be thought uncontrollable: automatic functions, such as heart activity, blood pressure, muscle tension, skin temperature, perspiration, and, perhaps, the activity of certain brain waves. Changes in some of these functions help to induce a physiological and mental state of calm and relaxation.

After being hooked up to a biofeedback computer with electrodes (painless noninvasive sensors) attached to your scalp, forehead, ear lobes, and hands, you try to manipulate tones, lights, or video characters on a computer screen that reflect various physiological functions. As you monitor your progress, you experiment with different breathing patterns, states of mind, visualization techniques, muscle states, and other aspects of the mind-body connection.

Once you learn how to reliably change particular functions while hooked up to the biofeedback equipment, you can use the strategies anywhere, any time to reduce stress and induce calm, thereby short-circuiting all kinds of problems. Biofeedback has proven useful for a host of conditions related to depression, including sleep disorders, tension and migraine headaches, anxiety, backache and other pain conditions, as well as phobias, addictions, and stress-related illnesses such as high blood pressure, asthma, ulcers, and bruxism (teeth clenching or grinding). Biofeedback practices are part of new field called applied psychophysiology.

Electroencephalographic or EEG biofeedback (also called neurofeedback), for example, monitors the activity of certain brain waves. Alpha waves, one type of brain waves, are more prevalent during relaxation, while beta waves are associated with alertness and attention. Using a video game–style program, you might try to change the display with your thoughts or other mental strategies to strengthen certain brain wave patterns.

Another kind of biofeedback improves functioning by improving the behavior of certain automatic regulatory processes. Respiratory sinus arrhythmia or RSA biofeedback involves learning to breathe lower in the abdomen and slower to increase heart rate variability. It has been shown to help reduce stress, blood pressure, and anxiety while improving mood and heart rate and rhythm. Once you master the exercise, continued conscious exercises are no longer necessary. (Interestingly, Indian psychiatrists recently reported that the breathing exercises of

Sudarshan Kriya Yoga significantly reduced the symptoms of dysthymia among the participants in a small study.)

An intriguing new area of research explores how some dimensions of brain-wave activity appear to correlate with cheerfulness/approach versus negativity/avoidance. Preliminary work suggests that people with greater alpha activity in their left frontal lobe than in their right tend to be cheerful and resilient while those with more activity in the right frontal lobe tend to be fretful and negative. Some evidence in this frontal brain asymmetry research suggests that to some extent the asymmetry may be reversed with EEG biofeedback. Researchers hope that through biofeedback training, you may be able produce a brain state that is less vulnerable to dysthymia and depression.

A typical course of biofeedback treatment is between 5 and 20 sessions of less than an hour each. Biofeedback is particularly effective when used with psychotherapy, so that you not only learn how to control your physiological response to stress, pain, and other triggers but also how to recognize and control your thoughts to influence your feelings that cause the high level of stress in the first place.

Eye Movement Desensitization and Reprocessing or EMDR

Eye movement desensitization and reprocessing (EMDR) is increasingly accepted as useful for posttraumatic stress and several other psychological disorders, including associated depression. The therapist asks the client to recall a distressing memory from the past and to visualize it in more and more detail as he or she watches the therapist's finger move back and forth. More recently, the therapy has expanded from just directed eye movements to other rhythmic moves such as finger tapping or musical tones. The technique also includes talking about the individual's feelings and thoughts when visualizing the upsetting event. The client learns how to recognize irrational assumptions and exaggerated concerns ("I can trust no one!"), and then how to visualize the event and reshape the feelings about it until the event isn't upsetting anymore, thus desensitizing the person to the past. Upsetting memories are worked on one at a time.

Although several dozen studies have explored EMDR's effectiveness, experts say most of them have been flawed and too short term to be conclusive. Nevertheless, a task force of the American Psychological Association reports that the technique is "probably efficacious." Its benefits, however, seem to be due more to its behavioral and cognitive techniques, especially desensitization than to activating particular brain regions via rhythmic movements. Therefore, we do not recommend it for treatment of dysthymia.

Massage and Music, but Turn Off the TV

Although neither massage nor music should be thought of as a treatment for dysthymia, both can serve as useful supplemental strategies as they can help promote relaxation, reduce stress, and perhaps even boost mood.

Music, for example, is widely acknowledged as being able to evoke emotion. Not surprisingly, many depressed people listen to music that focuses on sad themes, particularly romantic heartbreak. Donald Hodges, the director of the Institute for Music Research at the University of Texas at San Antonio, suggests that to help reduce depression, start with music that matches your mood and then move up gradually to something more upbeat.

Massage can help reduce muscle tension and promote pleasure, something that many people with dysthymia severely lack.

Watch as little television as possible. According to Martin Seligman at the University of Pennsylvania, surveys repeatedly show that the average mood of people watching sitcoms is one of a mild depression. Other research suggestions that television can exacerbate a pre-existing depression. In children, numerous studies show heavy television watching is linked to inactivity and obesity and obesity is linked to poor self-esteem and depression.

Religion and Spirituality

Religion can promote a sense of serenity, of purpose to life, of gratitude, and of intimacy with a higher power. A religious community can extend your support system and provide numerous opportunities for counseling, for social events, and for community service, which have been proven to help boost mood. (Helping others makes us feel useful, busy, and distracted and provides new social contacts and roles in life.) Having a religious or spiritual involvement may also help redirect some of the energy used on ourselves to others.

Researchers at the Human Population Laboratory in Berkeley, California who have studied the effects of religion on depression in those over 50, have found that while nonorganized religion had no effect on depression, organized religion in one's life helped reduce depression by buffering stress that's generated from outside the family. (Family stress, however, seemed to be exacerbated when the individuals had a religious affiliation.) Other studies have found that individuals who were religious tended to be less depressed than those who weren't.

Experimental Medical Treatments

Various treatments are being explored for major depression that probably do not have much applicability at this time for dysthymia. The preliminary studies under way are all focused on major depression, and treatments are expensive and not covered by insurance.

Repetitive Transcranial Magnetic Stimulation (rTMS).   Repetitive Transcranial Magnetic Stimulation (rTMS) involves the use of high-intensity magnetic pulses, which pass right through bone, daily for a week to stimulate the brain's left prefrontal cortex and the release of neurotransmitters. Preliminary work suggests that this may help some medication-resistant depressed patients without any side effects. There is some hope that rTMS may sometime replace electroconvulsive treatment.

Vagus Nerve Stimulation.   Vagus nerve stimulation (VNS), which is currently used as a treatment for epilepsy, involves electrically stimulating the left vagus nerve in the neck with a series of tiny electrical pulses generated from a small device in the chest. A small surgically implanted wire leads from the device to the vagus nerve which runs up through the neck to the brain. The vagus nerve is important for transmitting to the brain information that's relevant to mood, sleep, and other functions to the brain. According to a preliminary study conducted at Columbia University, University of Texas Southwestern Medical Center at Dallas, Baylor University, and the Medical University of South Carolina, about one-third of individuals studied who haven't responded to other forms of treatment for depression have responded well to VNS. This treatment thus holds hope as an alternative to electroconvulsive therapy for some patients.

Homeopathy.   Homeopathy refers to the use of tiny doses of medications and minerals, which would produce in healthy persons symptoms related to the disease, to try to subtly restore the balance of physiological systems. Homeopathy is not in the mainstream of medicine, and there is scant evidence that it offers anything over and above the nonspecific benefits of treatment. However, alternative practitioners use it widely. Its advantages are that it appears to do no harm: homeopathists take a lot of time interviewing their patients and tend to be very optimistic and positive about the effectiveness of the treatment, all of which are helpful. Depending on the cause of the depression and symptoms, common remedies include aurum metallicum, causticum, gelsemium, ignatia, and lachesis. It's difficult to determine how effective such therapy is without controlled double-blind studies; it's also difficult to assess the benefits of homeopathy because some of the beneficial effects reported may be due to the placebo effect.

Acupuncture.   Although few controlled studies have looked at the effectiveness of acupuncture, it too does no harm and at least one small study found acupuncture helpful in relieving depression in 64 percent of the women in the study.

Hypnosis.   Little if any research has looked at the applications of hypnosis for the treatment of depressive disorders. We do know of people who have used hypnosis to gain control over certain problematic behaviors, such as overeating, smoking, and insomnia. However, without any solid research, it's hard to recommend hypnosis when there are numerous effective alternatives.

Next, we will look at the special concerns of various populations in relation to dysthymia and mild depression.

PART THREE

◆ ◆ ◆

Special Concerns of Various Populations

11

◆ ◆ ◆

Dysthymia in Children, Adolescents, and Young Adults

People are always blaming their circumstances
for what they are. I don't believe in circumstances. The people who get on in this world
are the people who get up and look for the
circumstances they want, and, if they don't
find them, make them.

—George Bernard Shaw,
Mrs. Warren's Profession

We can not change our past. We can not
change the fact that people act in a certain
way. We can not change the inevitable. The
only thing we can do is play on the one string
we have, and that is our attitude.

—Charles R. Swindoll

Dysthymia afflicts children, too. In fact, the vast majority of adults—
some 75 percent—with dysthymia report that their mood difficulties
began while they were children or teenagers. Diagnosing dysthymia
early is important, not only to improve a child's quality of life but also
to prevent problems later in life. Depressed kids may be irritable and
act out, or they become passive and withdraw. They stop trying hard
and do poorly in school, don't connect much with other kids, are moody
and contrary, and later become promiscuous, rebellious or turn to ways
to self-medicate with alcohol or drugs. And, as in adulthood, suicidal
behavior can be a consequence of feeling stuck in a hopeless existence.
Although it is normal for adolescents to be moody, it is the broader,
all-encompassing, and persistent changes in mood and behavior that
distinguish dysthymia from normal moodiness.

According to various studies, about 3 percent of children have dysthymia at any one time, but the chance of any one child developing it sometime before age 18 is almost triple that rate. Only about 20 percent ever get treated, though, and, as a result, more than two-thirds of youngsters with dysthymia will develop major depression within several years; by their teens, 15 to 20 percent of adolescents have a major depressive episode. Life can be hard for kids who have little control over whether or not they are in an abusive relationship or will be a witness to violence, for example. The post-9/11 world of exploding airplanes and parking lot snipers can haunt a 10-year-old who doesn't have the coping skills an adult might have to counteract gloomy thoughts.

If children with dysthymia slip through the cracks—and many of them do, especially the ones who are getting by and doing okay in school although they seem a little depressed most of the time—many will later develop substance abuse problems to mute the symptoms. Chronic depression in adult life is the "natural" consequence of childhood-onset dysthymia. Early-onset depression also may foreshadow development of bipolar disorder.

With dysthymia (and major depression) badly underdiagnosed and undertreated in childhood and adolescence, many kids stumble as they try to navigate the developmental milestones of forming healthy social networks. Their ability to set goals and form identities can be impaired. Kids who are down are much more likely to avoid social contact or to be left out by other kids. This causes them to be even more dejected and isolated and less likely to develop good social skills. Because kids who are depressed, even mildly, can't concentrate and don't have much energy, they tend to do poorly in school, which can devastate their self-esteem and make them even sadder and more glum. The result is a youngster with few friends, an inadequate network of interpersonal relationships, more stress, and a dimmer future in terms of education and job opportunities. And when friendships are formed, there is the natural tendency for "birds of a feather . . ." This may result in a peer group that reinforces the sense of being on the outside looking in.

Dysthymia in Children

Among children, depression and dysthymia develop just about as often in boys as in girls. Although the symptoms of dysthymia are similar for children as for adults, children may be irritable rather than evidently down most of the day. In adults, symptoms need to persist most of the time for two years for dysthymia to be diagnosed; in children and adolescents, one year is adequate for a diagnosis. When a child is persistently irritable or depressed and has two other symptoms over this time period, they may meet the criteria for a diagnosis of dysthymia.

Is your child glum? unhappy? lonely? isolated? quiet? pessimistic? irritable?

Your child may have dysthymia if he or she is sad, down, or irritable on most days, and has two more symptoms—

- Doesn't enjoy activities they used to love
- Complains of headaches or stomachaches
- Does poorly in school
- Always seems bored
- Doesn't have much energy
- Can't concentrate
- Eating or sleeping patterns have changed

and these symptoms have persisted for one year.

ADHD

Attention Deficit Hyperactivity Disorder (ADHD) is the foremost problem for which children are referred to mental health clinicians, and it is now known to be closely linked to depression. Clinicians are finding evidence of depression or dysthymia in many kids with ADHD by the time they are 10 or 11; poor concentration, social difficulties, and sleep disturbances are hallmarks of both conditions. By age 25, the overwhelming percentage of those with ADHD have another mental health problem, and most of the time it is a depressive disorder. Dysthymia alone may be 10 times as common among adults with ADHD as in the general population.

Although ADHD in children gets a lot more publicity than it does in adults, many ADHD children never outgrow the condition as they age. When an adult with ADHD does not respond to an antidepressant, a doctor may recommend a trial of a stimulant, such as methylphenidate (Ritalin).

TREATMENT

Because kids with dysthymia seem to be sullen and pessimistic, cognitive-behavioral therapy can go a long way in teaching them how to challenge their negative ways of thinking. When therapy alone isn't effective enough, medication is often used, although the FDA has only approved Prozac for use in children and teens. The FDA warns, however, that a small percentage of youths, about 2 per 100, get more depressed when they take Prozac, and therefore stresses pursuing nonmedication treatments first in children and adolescents.

Dysthymia in Adolescents

Adolescence is a difficult time, even for the healthiest of children: hormones wreak havoc on moods while peer pressure, social exclusivity, academic pressures, increasing responsibilities, and sexual, gender, and identity issues can devastate self-esteem and trigger skyrocketing levels of stress and anxiety. Adolescence is a time to individualize, to discover what activities and subjects in school one likes and doesn't like, what kinds of friends one wants, what kind of identity one wants to have, and so on. Dysthymia can interfere with all these essential developmental milestones.

For all these reasons, adolescence is a particularly vulnerable period and teenagers are at particularly high risk for depression. Experts estimate that about 1 out of 20 adolescents will experience dysthymia; about 10 percent of these will develop a major depression within a year. By age 15, depression and dysthymia become twice as common in girls than in boys. The risk factors, just as in adults, include a genetic predisposition, having a parent who's depressed, stressful events, grief, anxiety, sexual abuse, and acting out.

Although mild depression may develop and just persist, dysthymia or its shorter form—subsyndromal depression—also is a common residual affect of major depression in adolescents. In other words, when major depression is not fully resolved, its milder but pernicious form—dysthymia—can linger for years, poisoning a young person's outlook and mental health and putting the youngster at a much higher risk for psychological problems, including major depression and suicide (the second leading cause of death among teens).

Cognitive and interpersonal forms of psychotherapy have been shown to be very effective for adolescents with dysthymia and should be considered a first-line therapy. If therapy is not adequate, a combination treatment of therapy with an antidepressant, is often recommended. SSRIs (serotonin reuptake inhibitors) are usually the first medications considered.

SPECIAL CONCERNS OF ADOLESCENTS

Keep in mind that adolescents often face concerns and conflicts that are different from those of adults. Commonly encountered problems include the following.

Stigma. In teens, there is often an unwillingness to take antidepressants because of the stigma. Clinicians also are reluctant to ask adolescents about their sex lives, which will lead to overlooking the sexual side effects that sometimes complicate SSRI therapy.

Smoking. Teenage years are most critical for vulnerability to smoking. University of Cincinnati College of Medicine researchers found that smoking was the "strongest predictor" for whether teenagers will develop depressive symptoms within a year.

Drug and alcohol abuse. The irritability, low self-esteem, social isolation, and lack of pleasure of dysthymia set the stage for drug use among teens. In the search for a "kick" or "up," teens may try amphetamines and other drugs.

Behavior problems. Youths who are depressed or dysthymic are more likely to behave in antisocial ways, rebelling against authority, neglecting homework, becoming delinquent.

Eating disorders and self-mutilation. Girls in particular express their low self-esteem and depressed feelings by trying to exert control over their bodies. Anorexia nervosa, bulimia, and self-cutting are all serious expressions of pain and despair, and girls who engage in these behaviors should seek immediate psychological and medical counseling.

Anxiety. The stress of school, social criticism, education challenges, learning disabilities, sexual identity—all these problems become exaggerated in teenagers and can all become risk factors for anxiety.

As with adults, getting treatment is critical for recovery from dysthymia. Treatment works in more than 80 percent of cases.

Children, in particular, who show signs of dysthymia or depression should get treatment as soon as possible. Learning as early as possible cognitive-behavioral skills and ways to calm themselves down can inoculate them from persistent negative thinking and anxiety when they mature into vulnerable teenagers. Other good ways to protect kids are to get them involved in exercise, sports, or other forms of physical activity, recreational activities they enjoy, community service, religious organizations, and other activities that interest and challenge them (see chapters 8 and 10 for other ideas).

College Students

Recently attention has been drawn to the increasing number of college students seeking treatment for depression—some schools report jumps of between 40 to 50 percent in the use of their counseling services since 1995 (and 17 to 22 percent spikes since 9/11). Depressive disorders are largely to blame. One study, for example, found that 14 percent of college students surveyed had significant depressive symptoms. That may be because there is more screening and recognition of the special stresses endured by college students or, in fact, because the pressures of college are getting to them. Those special stressors include

- Changes in eating and sleeping patterns
- Mounting academic pressures
- Sudden financial responsibilities
- Upheavals in social life
- Constant exposure to new people, ideas, and temptations
- Sudden lifestyle choices, including more intense sexual identity awareness
- Anxiety about life after graduation in a world changed by 9/11, a shrinking economy, and job scarcity

The good news is that more and more colleges are aware of the special vulnerability of college students to dysthymia and major depression and are well equipped to handle the problem—as long as students seek help.

12

♦ ♦ ♦

Gender and Dysthymia

Why Women Have a High Rate of Dysthymia

The fact that women have twice the rate of depression as men is a worldwide phenomenon. Some 9 percent of American women at any particular time suffer from some form of depression compared with less than half that of men. In fact, in at least one study, up to half the women surveyed said they'd had some kind of depression at some time in their lives.

Studies suggest a range of potential reasons for the gender differences, from women's cyclical hormonal changes and their ruminative style of thinking to their greater use of emotion-focused ways of coping, to their many psychosocial disadvantages compared with men. Whether genes account for the gender difference in depression is still not known.

Women are more likely to be abused, be subjugated, have less education, and hold lower-paying, lower status jobs than men. Women tend to have more role conflicts and stress, less independence, less control over their lives, and lower self-esteem than men. Women are less able to defend themselves physically and are more likely to be poor and experience humiliations in life than men. They also tend to more frequently fret about their weight, their children, and other relationships than men do. Even when women are successful in life, they tend to have a lot more stress trying to juggle their multiple roles as wife, mother, and wage earner.

HORMONAL EVENTS AND DEPRESSION

We know from a host of studies that the risk of depression increases with the various changes in sex hormones caused by puberty, premenstrual syndrome (PMS), pregnancy, childbirth (including postpartum), menopause, and the use of birth control pills. It is now clear that irregularities in the body's supply of estrogen and other hormones (women are also more likely than men to develop low thyroid problems) alter the activity of neurotransmitters such as serotonin. These life events that involve changes in hormone levels and brain activity not only affect mood, sleep, and irritability but also may make women more sensitive to psychosocial stresses.

Many depressive episodes correlate with hormonal events in women's lives.

Puberty.   Girls who get their first periods before age 11 are more likely to develop depression during adolescence than girls who mature later. All girls, however, face an increased risk of depression after puberty.

Women in their childbearing years.   This group of women is at highest risk for the onset of depression, with almost 20 percent of women between the ages of 20 to 45 suffering from depression at some time. Depression before each month's menstrual period (premenstrual dysphoric disorder) afflicts up to 8 percent of women in this age group and puts women at a much higher risk for major depression and dysthymia.

Contraceptives.   Up to 10 percent of women who take birth control pills experience depressive symptoms. When asked in medical or mental health exams about medications (since many medications can exacerbate depressive symptoms), women often neglect to mention contraceptives, as many don't regard them as "medication."

Postpartum depression.   Up to 20 percent of new mothers suffer from some form of depression, especially those with a history of depressive problems, with babies who have medical problems, or with little social support.

Pregnancy and nursing.   Women have to consider the safety of antidepressants if they are pregnant or nursing. Although some physicians in general discourage the use of any medications, if possible, during these periods, research so far suggests that taking SSRIs or tricyclic antidepressants appears to be safe during pregnancy.

Miscarriage and abortion. These events similarly increase the risk for depression, especially for women with no children, and for women with a history of depression.

Menopause. As the body eases into menopause, the hormonal changes coupled with the other problems associated with aging triggers depressive symptoms in many women, especially those with a personal or family history of depression. Women with problem marriages, financial difficulties, divorce, and empty nests are also at higher risk.

Although menopause per se doesn't seem to be a risk factor in women with no history of depression, many of the changes of menopause are similar to depression, including cognitive changes, irritability, fatigue, sleep problems, and loss of libido. In women with no history of depression, these changes are usually due to the hormonal changes of menopause, not to a depression.

In addition to changes in estrogen levels during menopause, which dampen serotonin levels, women in menopause also tend to experience increases in monoamine oxidase, decreases in cortisol, and decreases in other hormones, all of which may contribute to a higher risk of depression.

Postmenopause. During this period, women's depression rates seem to go down until they become elderly (see chapter 13). Interestingly, the vast difference in rates of depression between men and women decline as they age, until the rates actually become fairly equal in very old age. Some research suggests that postmenopausal women don't respond to SSRIs (selective serotonin reuptake inhibitors) as younger women do, and some researchers are looking into using larger doses or different medications to treat depression in older women.

SEX AND THYROID HORMONES

Estrogen and progesterone, the major female sex hormones, are vital components to a woman's well-being. While estrogen promotes blood flow and increases serotonin activity in the brain, it also must be balanced by progesterone.

Estrogen appears to affect those very brain neurotransmitters that may influence mood by preventing the breakdown and promoting the production of serotonin and by boosting the number and sensitivity of serotonin receptors in the brain, both of which help increase the amount of serotonin in the brain. When estrogen plummets before the onset of menses each month, just after childbirth, and with the onset of menopause, a woman becomes much more vulnerable to depression and mood disorders. Men, on the other hand, do not experience these fluctuations. In addition, both culture and higher levels of testosterone may help protect mood by promoting more active coping behaviors.

Women are at much higher risk for thyroid problems. Too little thyroid hormone not only can lower your threshold for depression but can cause sluggishness and a lack of energy and alertness. When hypothyroidism is present, it is difficult to treat depression without also providing thyroid hormone replacement.

PSYCHOSOCIAL FACTORS

Compared with men, women have a lot more psychosocial risk factors when it comes to dysthymia. Women are

- More likely to have been abused as children and adults and then more likely to be a victim of repeated abuse
- More vulnerable to stressful events (women seem to be three times more vulnerable to depression after stressful events than men are)
- More likely to engage in ruminative thinking, mulling over and over the possible causes and consequences of their distress
- More sensitive to relationship problems, which readily affect their self-concept and sense of self-worth
- Under more stress, juggling their roles as caregivers to children and parents, wife, worker, and volunteer
- Less educated, earn less income, and receive fewer job promotions; tend to experience more discrimination and tend to have lower social, economic, and political status, poorer housing, less financial security
- More vulnerable because of gender differences in their views of the meaning of marriage and children: Whereas marriage seems to protect men from depression, studies show that it does not appear to provide any protection against depression for women. One view is that because women are better sources of social support, a married man usually has at least one supportive person in his life.

Women are more likely than men to be coping as single parents. A 2002 study from the Royal College of Psychiatrists in Cardiff, Great Britain, found that single mothers are three times more likely to be depressed than other women.

In addition, the World Health Organization reported in 1996 that married women with children had higher depression rates than married childless women, single women, or men. Rates of depression among mothers seem to diminish somewhat as their children get older: mothers caring for toddlers and grandmothers caring for grandchildren have higher rates of depression.

It's interesting to note that in some cultural groups that don't have the conflicting roles for women, such as the Amish, rates of depression for men and women are much more equal.

Lesbians and minority women are also at higher risk for depression—probably because of the respective social stigma and economic constraints.

STYLES OF THINKING

Does a woman's style of thinking put her at higher risk for dysthymia? Although this may sound like a generalization or stereotype, it is true.

Girls and women are more likely to feel disempowered, a phenomenon psychologists have called learned helplessness. They aren't taught to be as self-reliant as boys are.

Girls are less likely to distract themselves with physical labor, working out, watching or playing sports, going out, etc., when overcome with strong emotions. Although men tend to bottle up their feelings—whether they are too ashamed or too embarrassed to discuss them—their active avoidance tends to block feelings of sadness. Women, on the other hand, tend to ruminate, think about their problems constantly, analyze them, and dwell on them.

PURSUIT OF THINNESS

Almost every woman knows the comfort of chocolate, cake, or ice cream when one is down. Many women also know the agony of feeling too fat and the lifelong struggle to be thin. Women are twice as likely to be "on a diet" at any given time; ironically, this is very close to the gender difference in rates of depression in the United States. No matter how hard women try to diet, the struggle for thinness tends to increase problems with dysthymia and depression, says Dr. Martin Seligman of the University of Pennsylvania. This is because you can't control your weight as much as you'd like. You feel insecure about your body and you are constantly reminded of your failure (with mirrors, temptations, advertisements, movie stars). All these "failures" contribute to a loss of self-esteem.

Interestingly, boys and girls have the same rates of depression and dysthymia, but after puberty, when girls are more concerned about appearance and dieting, girls end up with higher rates of depression than boys.

Women are more likely to overeat when they're depressed than men, which triggers a vicious, repeating cycle of more weight gain, lower self-esteem, and then the tendency to eat because of persistent depression.

Men and Dysthymia

"The mass of men lead lives of quiet desperation. What is called resignation is confirmed desperation."

—Henry David Thoreau

Although more than twice as many women than men develop dysthymia, that's not to say that many men aren't miserable, too. Men, however, are far less likely than women to do anything about it. Perhaps that's because men tend to be less comfortable than women talking about their feelings, or may be too embarrassed or ashamed to admit their sadness, or may view their inability to reap pleasure from life or their chronic state of the blues as a personal weakness rather than a disease. Many men just won't talk about their despair. From the outside their life seems okay. They don't understand why on the inside there are hovering clouds of sadness, bleakness, or passivity.

Rather than crying or ruminating about their despondency as some women do, or talking or thinking about it as other women do, men tend to distract themselves by staying busy—immersing themselves in work or exercise. As they deny their sadness, they may become irritable, angry, withdrawn, or act out in inappropriate ways. They may mask their depressive feelings and try to make themselves feel more alive with addictions or aggression—by drinking or doing drugs, womanizing, overeating, or overspending, getting into fights, experiencing road rage, taking off in their cars or motorcycles.

While some men withdraw from their close relationships, others lash out in anger. Their mild forms of depression can have severe consequences—chronic depression can destroy their marriages, hurt their children, and waste their lives.

Some researchers point out that men are more likely to mask their depression by drinking. In cultures that don't use alcohol—such as Amish and Orthodox Jewish communities—the incidence of depression is about the same in men as in women.

MEN AND TREATMENT

Just as in women, psychotherapy and antidepressant medication each work about 50 percent of the time for men; in combination, they work about 80 percent of the time. However, many researchers suggest that an effective mode of treatment for men is to focus on doing what they think would make them feel better—spending more time with the family, helping out more at home—even if they don't feel like it. As we said in chapter 5, the feelings will follow the behavior.

Several studies have looked at the value of testosterone in men with dysthymia. In one study of HIV-positive men with depression or dysthymia, for example, the group that took testosterone did just as well as those on standard antidepressants. And in a 2002 study of older men from the New York State Psychiatric Institute, researchers reported that those with dysthymia have significantly lower levels of testosterone than men with major depression or men with no depressive symptoms. As discussed in the previous section on women, this work suggests that the sex hormones may play a larger role in dysthymia than previously thought. Both mild depression and mild hormonal dysfunction are widely undiagnosed in older men.

Gay Men and Women

Gay men are particularly vulnerable to depression and dysthymia, say the experts, probably because of the stress of coping in a straight world, of dealing with families and co-workers, of coming out or staying in the closet, of avoiding or living with HIV and gay bashing. All of this takes its toll. Gay men also have a higher risk of contracting HIV/AIDS and, once infected, are at a much higher risk for dysthymia: of those who are HIV-positive, up to one-quarter have dysthymia, according to a UCLA survey of 2,900 HIV-positive adults; and about one-third have major depression. Whether or not gay men are HIV-positive, however, if they are dysthymic, they evidently are at almost twice the risk for engaging in unsafe sex in the previous six months, according to a 2000 study at Adelaide University, Australia. Whereas major depression is linked to lack of sexual drive, dysthymia is more linked to low self-esteem, passivity, and a lack of caring.

Another note of particular interest for anyone with HIV is that the common herbal remedy, St. John's wort, which is commonly used for mild depression, interferes with the effectiveness of many medications, including Crixivan (indinavir) and other protease inhibitors used to treat HIV infection. See chapter 9 for other medications known to be seriously affected by St. John's wort.

13

♦ ♦ ♦

Dysthymia and Aging

Shines the last age, the next with hope is seen,
Today slinks poorly off unmarked between:
Future or Past no richer secret folds,
O friendless Present! than thy bosom holds.

—Ralph Waldo Emerson

Dysthymia and Depression
in the Elderly

Dysthymia and other forms of depression are the leading mental health problems in older adults but they are highly treatable. In fact, from one-fifth to one-third of those over 65 (depending on which survey you read) will suffer from some sort of depression, but only a fraction will get treatment for it.

• About one-quarter of older adults suffer from subsyndromal depression (two to three symptoms of dysthymia or depression rather than five or more, either short term or long term).

• About 15 percent of all older adults—twice as many women as men—suffer from dysthymia and other forms of mild depression. Some researchers, however, see the rates of dysthymia begin to balance more equally between the genders in the older population.

• More than one-half of older adults who live with illnesses or in nursing homes suffer from some form of depression. Among these elders, dysthymia is as common as major depression.

Why older adults are more likely to be blue
Limited incomes
Poor housing
Social isolation, loneliness
Sight, hearing, and mobility problems
Family communication problems
Grief over loss of spouse and other loved ones
Caregiving responsibilities
Coping with a chronic illnesses, pain, and disability

Many conditions that afflict the elderly are associated with depression—Alzheimer's disease, Parkinson's disease, multiple sclerosis, thyroid disorders, diabetes, kidney and liver disease, dementia, pancreatic cancer, adrenal disorders, heart failure and heart attack, stroke, and vitamin B12 deficiency. Generally, the older you get, the more likely you are to be hospitalized for some illness and to suffer a loss of body image from aging, surgical scars, or even amputation.

Older adults who are less mobile feel less in control of their lives and more helpless. They find themselves unable to do favorite things, such as sewing, playing tennis or golf, or driving a car, because of their physical impairments. Their impairments also make them more fearful of and vulnerable to street crime. And, they think about facing their death more often than younger people do.

Biochemically, the elderly have a different profile than they had when they were younger as well. They generally have lower levels of neurotransmitters. The level of serotonin in an 80-year-old seems to be about half that in a 60-year-old. Older adults also are more likely to be taking certain medications known to have depression as a possible side effect: for example, beta-adrenergic blockers and digitalis (for heart conditions), histamine H2-receptor antagonists (for ulcers), metoclopramide (Reglan) to improve digestion. (See chapter 3 for a more complete list of medications that may have depressive side effects.)

Researchers also point out that older brains are less pliant and adaptable and less responsive to medication. A middle-aged woman taking antidepressant medication may feel its effects in about three weeks, but an older woman typically doesn't feel any relief for 12 weeks or longer.

At particularly high risk for depression are older adults living in nursing homes who suffer from chronic or disabling disorders, those in mourning, and those caring for chronically ill spouses. To make matters worse, depression and dysthymia can exacerbate pain. Illnesses such as stroke, Parkinson's disease, heart or lung disease, and fractures are more debilitating for the elderly and can lead to depression. And when depression is chronic, it may significantly compromise one's immune system. Depressive disorders also increase the risk of suicide: older adults have triple the risk of suicide as younger people. The rates of suicide in older white men are higher than all the other age and sex groups. On the positive side, some research shows that treatment for depression can improve the functional status of older adults.

Symptoms of Dysthymia in Older Adults

Although the symptoms of dysthymia in older adults are the same as in younger people, we may not recognize them as readily in older people, perhaps because we mistakenly assume that symptoms such as fatigue, insomnia, and poor concentration are part of old age. Seniors may be dysthymic if they

- Don't get pleasure from the things that used to bring them joy
- Don't show interest in hobbies and other forms enjoyable activities
- Are withdrawn
- Complain excessively of minor physical problems, such as gas, constipation, heartburn, pain, fatigue
- Have sleeping and eating problems
- Are irritable
- Have problems remembering, concentrating, making decisions
- Are passive—don't bother to cook, eat, or take prescribed medication
- Feel hopeless, don't care if they die
- Have no sense of purpose
- Feel worthless, have low self-esteem
- Shuffle through days apathetically with little vitality, energy, or pleasure but a great deal of uncertainty, detachment, and emptiness
- Despair that time is running out
- Say things like "I don't want to bother," "That's too much trouble," "I don't feel up to it," "I don't have the energy." Too often, such expressions are taken at face value rather than as signs of depression.

Some of these symptoms may indeed indicate serious medical (biological, physiological or biochemical) problems or changes, but they also may be symptoms of dysthymia, a treatable psychological condition and not as the inevitable sign of aging either.

UNDERDIAGNOSED AND UNDERTREATED

Despite skyrocketing rates of dysthymia and depression in the elderly, up to 90 percent of depression in the elderly goes untreated, reports The National Institute of Mental Health (NIMH).

Why Dysthymia or Depression Is Harder to Recognize in Seniors

- It can develop so gradually—often after an illness or death of a loved one—that it's never identified as depression or dysthymia.

- Many people wrongly believe that feeling depressed later in life is normal.

- Instead of showing sadness and withdrawal, older adults may be irritable, apathetic, or only report physical problems, such as aches and pains.

- Complaints about constipation, heartburn, insomnia, lack of appetite, aches, pains, and so on are often dismissed as hypochondria rather than as possible signs of depression.

- Older people take many medications (on average, ranging from 2 to 18 different medications), and it's difficult to distinguish whether certain symptoms are side effects of medications or are symptoms of depression.

- Many older people are chronically ill, disabled, or show signs of other mental health problems, such as confusion, agitation, anxiety, or of disorders such as Parkinson's or Alzheimer's disease, dementia, and thyroid disorders, so that symptoms of depression may be masked.

- Many older people refuse to talk about their feelings.

- Many older people may be too ashamed to admit their depression or believe that nothing can be done about it anyway.

Because dysthymia and other forms of mild depression are vastly underdiagnosed, they are vastly undertreated. As in younger adults, dysthymia can ruin a life and perhaps even lead to its end. Although older Americans comprise only 13 percent of the population, they account for 20 percent of the suicides. In fact, an older person with suicidal thoughts is five times more likely to complete suicide than a younger person with suicidal thoughts. (These statistics don't take into account other ways that older people may hasten death, such as not eating, taking medications irregularly, or not participating in other treatment).

Because older people who are depressed often see their doctor (as they have higher rates of accidents and medical problems), usually to complain of physical problems—many may be hospitalized (costing society billions of dollars) when therapy for depression might be more effective. People who are depressed tend to stay in the hospital longer and take longer to recover from illnesses and surgery. Depression also worsens the course of certain diseases, such as heart and other cardiovascular problem.

Treatment of Dysthymia in Older Adults

As in other adults, the ideal treatment for dysthymia may be a combination of psychotherapy and antidepressants. However, to avoid adding another medication to a long roster of pills, some experts suggest trying psychotherapy first. The problem here is that many older people have been brought up to keep personal problems to themselves and are not accustomed to sharing their feelings. Many older adults may also avoid pursing therapy because their health insurance doesn't cover it.

Just receiving attentive care seems to have therapeutic effects—some researchers have found that bimonthly office visits to a physician plus a placebo pill can be just as effective as paroxetine (Paxil) or short-term behavioral therapy for mild depression and dysthymia in older adults.

What seems most effective in the elderly, recent research suggests, however, is that antidepressant medication is more effective than either therapy or a placebo in older adults with mild depression.

MEDICATION

One rule of thumb is to wait a month or two before actively treating mild depression in older adults and, in the meantime, try to improve the support system and encourage the person in question to pursue activities that bring pleasure or boost mood, such as exercise (see below). For dysthymia, however, starting medication at a low dose and having it increased slowly may be the way to go. Older adults need to increase their doses slowly because they often need less medication than younger adults and are more prone to side effects. One of the biggest problems among older adults, however, is compliance: research suggests that up to three-quarters of older adults don't take their medication as prescribed. Also, some research suggests that older people with chronic depression take longer to recover and have relapses sooner than younger adults. Older adults—especially older women—may respond slowly to antidepressant treatments compared to younger adults.

As for which medications, tricyclic antidepressants are just as effective as selective serotonin reuptake inhibitors (SSRIs) and relatively inexpensive, *but* they are much more apt to cause adverse side effects, so an SSRI, such as citalopram (Celexa) or sertraline (Zoloft) is usually a better choice. The SSRIs have been shown in double-blind studies to be effective and well tolerated for minor depression in elderly individuals.

Previously, physicians had to be more cautious about the use of antidepressants with the elderly because of potential problems with cardiovascular effects (such as low blood pressure upon standing or delayed cardiac conduction) or other side effects (such as constipation, urinary retention, or delirium). These concerns are far less relevant with modern antidepressants such as the SSRIs. In fact, several of the SSRIs, such as sertraline, citalopram, and escitalopram, even have a very low potential of interacting with other medications.

If an SSRI is not effective, new medications, such as mirtazapine (Remeron) or venlafaxine (Effexor), are useful. If a tricyclic is considered, most experts suggest nortriptyline (Aventyl).

A precaution: An SSRI may not be a good choice for those with Parkinson's disease since these medications may increase the risk of tremors and other symptoms of the disease. Individuals with cardiovascular disease or an enlarged prostate need to be sure their antidepressant does not aggravate their condition or increase their problems with urinary retention.

More than most other people, older people should be monitored regularly once they begin antidepressant medication. Side effects need to be dealt with promptly (often by switching medication), and if they have no effect in four or six weeks, another medication may be tried. Without regular checkups, the patient is much more likely to just stop taking the medication (that tremendous problem of poor compliance again). The elderly commonly take several medications and experience a variety of side effects, which may prompt them to be reluctant to take (or to stop taking) any additional medications, such as antidepressants, that they may view as not being critical to their health.

EXERCISE

Launching an exercise program at the first hint of mild depression or dysthymia is a good idea for so many reasons, but the most important reason is that it really works to boost mood. When compared with medication, walking at 70 to 85 percent of maximal aerobic intensity—that's about how it would feel to breathe while swimming or biking at a moderate rate—has been found to be just as effective as taking an SSRI. In one study, the exercise was a group activity. Although, in other studies, exercising individually has shown to significantly boost mood, groups can do double duty by also providing support and social contact.

Also proven effective with older people is supervised weight and strength training, aerobics, or stretching and relaxation exercises for those with physical limitations. So effective are the various exercise programs that many health insurance policies will cover the costs of health clubs or senior fitness programs provided by hospitals, churches, or community centers.

RELIGION

Whereas older people may not be as comfortable talking about their feelings as younger people are, many have been brought up to be religious, which may help them cope with all forms of adversity, including depression. According to at least one study, when older depressed patients had a stronger sense of faith, they responded better to treatment than patients who were rated as having little sense of faith. Interestingly, it was faith, *not* church going, that made the different.

CREATIVE PURSUITS

Because older people often have more leisure time, a good supplement to the strategies described above is the pursuit of creative endeavors, from watercolor painting and gardening to hobbies and talents that once were pursued. These kinds of activities can distract a person from their self-destructive ruminating thoughts as well as empower them with a sense of accomplishment, enhanced sense of control, and boost in self-esteem.

SOCIAL SUPPORT

Expanding one's social support network—by joining a book group, having a regular bridge game, attending church groups, going bowling—can provide critical social contacts. If a person is homebound because of caregiving responsibilities, respite care is essential. If a person is homebound because of physical limitations, computer access to groups and individuals can be a tremendous benefit and can go a long way to help a person feel connected with others.

♦ ♦ ♦

Conclusion:
Putting It All Together

The purpose of life is a life
of purpose.

—Robert Byrne

Yesterday is history
Tomorrow is a mystery
Today is a gift . . .
That is why it is
called the present

—Author unknown

If you believe that your life is lousy or you are glum and negative more
often than not, the easiest thing to do is nothing. But then nothing
will change. You can be sure of that.

The persistent and pervasive negativity and stress of dysthymia will
wither the spirit and will sap your vitality. But you don't *have* to live
that way.

*The good news is that just the act of pursuing some kind of treatment,
even self-help—will make you feel better automatically, because just taking
a constructive step and acting purposefully is very therapeutic.* Studies have
proven, time and again, that having a purpose combats persistent pessimism and forges the way toward a more hopeful, optimistic response.
Hopeful optimists are extremely unlikely to get depressed.

Regardless of how you decide to help yourself—be it a physical con-
ditioning program, an alternative health regimen, psychotherapy, or
doctor-prescribed antidepressants—remember that recovery is a process. Change is often slow, perhaps even imperceptible at times. Setbacks are common. But what's the alternative? *If you remain indifferent
to your passivity and pessimism, which are so natural to dysthymia, you will
make yourself miserable.*

Indifference is paralysis. It dooms you to a gray, flat life. The key to
finding your way out of flatness toward brightness and vitality is in

how you talk to yourself, keeping your attention focused on the present, knowing your purpose, accepting reality, and doing what has to be done—whether you feel like it or not.

Modern psychotherapists and psychiatrists are finding, after years of research, that they agree with the wisdom of the ages that a key to mental health (peace of mind, enlightenment, or whatever you want to call it) is to be mindful—living in the moment and being constructive, positive, and compassionate in your responses. All of the cognitive-behavioral therapies—and the ancient wisdom of the sages—draw upon these principles as the path to mental well-being.

To recap:

1. *Stay in the present.*   Today really is the first day of the rest of your life. Some suffering is part of life. Reality tells us that the past is over and the future hasn't happened yet, so the only opportunity we have is in the present. Regardless of your emotions, keep your attention on the moment.

2. *Accept the present circumstances and accept your feelings.* Acceptance doesn't mean that you like something—the terrorist attack, a disabling accident, the death of someone you loved, unemployment, a bad diagnosis—but to realize that since you can't change the circumstances that have occurred, switch your attention to deciding what you will do next. Respond with purpose. Acknowledge but do not dwell in the emotional reaction (regret, grief, anxiety, anger, fear). Acceptance is the only place from which any lasting health emerges. The way to do this is to practice observing your feelings and to realize that feelings don't have to be fixed, no matter how strong. Feelings are for feeling. Don't worry about trying to change them.

3. *Focus your attention on what you* can *control.*   Your thoughts, which create an either optimistic and positive or pessimistic and negative attitude, and your behavior. Thoughts create and sustain the attitude that shapes your behavior.

4. *Monitor your thoughts.*   When you are feeling depressed, fearful, angry, resentful, or jealous, *listen* to yourself.
   What are you telling yourself? Are you dwelling on something negative or creating distressful, insecure thoughts? Are you seeing only black and white? Are you making assumptions about what others are thinking or what will happen in the future? Are

you interpreting external reality accurately? Do you automatically respond in these kinds of ways, and do they tend to make you upset and stuck?

Catch yourself when you are ruminating, exaggerating, minimizing, overgeneralizing, or assuming you know what others think or feel. This style of thinking fosters depression. Challenge the validity of your thoughts. Could you see it another way? How would you suggest to a friend in the same circumstances that maybe there's another way to see things, that maybe it's not so bad or sad. And if it is that bad or sad, what are the chances that the worst case scenario will occur?

Recognizing what you are telling yourself is a crucial first step.

5. *Choose to respond rather than react.*   Responding and reacting are two totally different approaches. The only way lasting change will occur is to change your behavior in the present moment. Since responding emotionally doesn't offer a way out of hard times, but your behavior does (i.e., purposeful responses), think about what it is you really want to achieve. Keep your focus on the present and on your purpose.

Ask yourself, "What does external reality call for?" Weigh the benefits and risks of your next action clearly. Then respond purposefully with your full attention.

Attitude

"Words can never adequately convey the incredible impact of our attitude toward life. The longer I live the more convinced I become that life is 10 percent what happens to us and 90 percent how we respond to it.

"I believe the single most significant decision I can make on a day-to-day basis is my choice of attitude. It is more important than my past, my education, my bankroll, my successes or failures, fame or pain, what other people think of me or say about me, my circumstances, or my position. Attitude keeps me going or cripples my progress. It alone fuels my fire or assaults my hope."

—Charles R. Swindoll, *Strengthening Your Grip*,
used by permission of Insight for Living, Plano, Texas

You have the choice and the control to think your way to a healthy constructive response instead of reacting emotionally.

Life doesn't create depression, stress, anxiety, fear, and insecurity. Our interpretations and responses do. If *you* don't create your responses, your life will just drift without purpose. Creating your response is 100 percent in your control. Your feelings will change with your behavior. Change your behavior and your mood will improve, your feelings will brighten.

When you purposefully redirect your attention toward taking constructive action in the present, even in situations you don't like, you *will* feel better.

You don't have to feel good to respond well. Responding well will make you feel good.

You change by changing what you do—now.

One step at a time.

Take that step.

Then the next one, whether you feel like it or not.

That will make you feel better.

$\blacklozenge \quad \blacklozenge \quad \blacklozenge$

Appendices

APPENDIX 1

Daily Symptom Log							
At the end of each day, indicate each feeling you had for a significant part of the day and rate its severity or frequency on a scale of 1 to 5 (5 being most severe or most of day).							
	M	**T**	**W**	**Th**	**F**	**Sat**	**Sun**
Difficulty concentrating							
Repeated same problem thoughts							
Tired							
Irritable							
Felt little pleasure							
Trouble sleeping							
Eating a lot/a little							
Glum/down							
No energy, no exercise							
Felt socially withdrawn							
Self-critical							
No motivation							
Agitated							
Trouble making decisions							
Felt hopeless/helpless							

Commonly Used Antidepressants for Dysthymia

Brand Name of Commonly Used Antidepressants	Generic Name	Usual Dose mg/day	Type	Comments: Side effects + (least severe) to ++++ (most severe)								
				GI	Insom-nia	Weight Gain	Seda-tion	Libido	Head-ache	Dry Mouth	Dizzi-ness	
Prozac, Sarafem	fluoxetine	20–80	SSRI[a]	+	++			+	+			
Zoloft	sertraline	50–200	SSRI	++			+	+				Possibly loose stools, widely used in elderly, may help with hot flashes
Paxil	paroxetine	20–50	SSRI	+	+	+	+	++		+		Possibly dry mouth, constipation
Luvox	fluvoxamine	50–300	SSRI	++	+	+		++				Expensive, may help with hot flashes
Lexapro	escitalopram	10–20	SSRI	+	+		++	+	+			Widely used in elderly
Celexa	citalopram	20–40	SSRI	+	+		+	+				
Effexor	venlafaxine	75–375	SNRI[b]	++	+			+		++		May help with hot flashes. See note[d]
Cymbalta	duloxetine	40–60	SNRI	++	++							
Wellbutrin, Zyban	bupropion	75–400	NDRI[b]	+	+					+		
Serzone	nefazodone	200–600	Other[c]		+		+					
Remeron	mirtazapine	15–60	Other[c]			+	+++					

		150–500	Other[c]			++			
Desyrel	trazodone								
Elavil, Endep	amitriptyline	75–300	tricyclic	+	++	+	+++	+++	Can be deadly in overdose
Sinequan, Adapin	doxepin	75–300	tricyclic	+	++	+	+++	+++	Can be deadly in overdose
Tofranil, SK-Pramine	imipramine	25–100	tricyclic	+	++	+	+++	+++	Can be deadly in overdose
Norpramin, Pertofrane	desipramine	25–300	tricyclic	+	++	++	++	+++	Can be deadly in overdose
Pamelor, Aventyl	nortriptyline	50–150	tricyclic	+	++	+	++	+	Can be deadly in overdose
Vivactil	protriptyline	15–60	tricyclic	+	++	+	+++	+	Can be deadly in overdose
Anafranil	clomipramine	25–250	tricyclic	+	++	++	++	+++	Can be deadly in overdose
Surmontil	trimipramine	50–100	tricyclic	+	++	+++	++	+	Can be deadly in overdose
Marplan	isocarboxazid	20–60	MAO[e] inhibitor	+++	++		++	+++	MAOI diet
Nardil	phenelzine	15–90	MAO inhibitor	+++	++		++	+++	MAOI diet
Parnate	tranyl-cypromine	30–60	MAO inhibitor	+++	++		++	+++	MAOI diet

[a]SSRI: Selective serotonin reuptake inhibitor.
[b]This newer generation of antidepressants also inhibits the reuptake of norepinephrine (SNRI) and dopamine (NDRI).
[c]These antidepressants work through complex mechanisms that regulate the interaction of neurons controlling serotonin and norepinephrine neurons.
[d]May have stronger antidepressant effects than other newer antidepressants, but can increase blood pressure at higher doses.
[e]MAOI: Monoamine oxidase inhibitor.

APPENDIX 3
Resources

Organizations

American Academy of Child and Adolescent Psychiatry
3615 Wisconsin Avenue, N.W.
Washington, DC 20016
202-966-7300
http://www.aacap.org

American Institute for Cognitive Therapy
136 East 57th Street, Suite 1101
New York, NY 10022
212-308-2440
http://www.cognitivetherapynyc.com

American Psychiatric Association
1400 K Street, N.W.
Washington, DC 20005
202-682-6000
http://www.psych.org

American Psychiatric Nurses Association
1555 Wilson Boulevard, Suite 515
Arlington, VA 22209
703-243-2443
http://www.apna.org

American Psychological Association
750 First Street, N.E.
Washington, DC 20002
202-336-5500
http://www.apa.org

Association for the Advancement of Behavior Therapy
305 Seventh Avenue, 16th Floor
New York, NY 10001
212-647-1890 or 800-685-AABT
http://www.aabt.org

Beck Institute for Cognitive Therapy and Research
GSB Building, Suite 700
City Line and Belmont Avenues
Bala Cynwyd, PA 19004-1610
610-664-3020
http://www.beckinstitute.org/about.htm
E-mail: beckinst@gim.net

Child & Adolescent Bipolar Foundation
1187 Wilmette Avenue, PMB #331
Wilmette, IL 60091
847-256-8525
http://www.bpkids.org

Constructive Living

An educational approach to mental health based on two Japanese psychotherapies that are described in the books written by David K. Reynolds. Titles include *Constructive Living* and *A Handbook for Constructive Living* (both published by the University of Hawaii Press). More snippets of wisdom from *Constructive Living* may be found at: http://boat.zero.ad.jp/zbe85163, www.constructiveliving.ca, and www.constructiveliving.com.

Depressed Anonymous
502-569-1989
http://www.depressedanon.com

An international group that sponsors a 12-step program to help depressed persons; newsletter, phone support, information and referrals, workshops, conferences, seminars.

Depression Awareness, Recognition, and Treatment (D/ART) Program
See National Institute of Mental Health

DRADA (Depression and Related Affective Disorders Association)
Contact: DRADA, Meyer 3-181
600 North Wolfe Street
Baltimore, MD 21287-7381.
410-955-4647 or 202-955-5800
Fax: 410-614-3241.
www.drada.org
E-mail: drada@welchlink.welch.jhu.edu

Emotions Anonymous
P.O. Box 4245
St. Paul, MN 55104
612-647-9712
http://www.EmotionsAnonymous.org

Offers a 12-step program to help people experiencing emotional difficulties; has 1,400 groups worldwide.

National Alliance for the Mentally Ill
Colonial Place Three
2107 Wilson Boulevard, Suite 300
Arlington, VA 22201-3042
703-524-7600
Fax: 703-516-7238
http://www.nami.org/pressroom

A nonprofit, grassroots, self-help, support, and advocacy organization of consumers, families, and friends of people with severe mental illnesses (schizophrenia, major depression, bipolar disorder, obsessive-compulsive disorder, anxiety disorders).

National Association of Social Workers
750 First Street, N.E., Suite 700
Washington, DC 20002-4201
202-408-8600
http://www.socialworkers.org

National Center for Complementary and Alternative Medicine
NCCAM Clearinghouse
P.O. Box 7923
Gaithersburg, MD 20898
888-644-6226
International: 301-519-3153
TTY: 866-464-3615
http://nccam.nih.gov/health/clearinghouse
E-mail: info@nccam.nih.gov

Dedicated to exploring complementary and alternative healing practices in the context of rigorous science, training CAM researchers, and disseminating authoritative information to the public and professionals.

National Depressive and Manic-Depressive Association (NDMDA)
730 North Franklin Street, Suite 501
Chicago, IL 60610-3526
800-826-3632 or 800-82-NDMDA or 312-642-0049
http://www.ndmda.org

Makes referrals to local support services and offers a free information package.

National Foundation for Depressive Illness
P.O. Box 2257
New York, NY 10016
800-239-1265
212-268-4260
http://www.depression.org

National Institute of Mental Health (NIMH)
5600 Fishers Lane, Room 10-85
Rockville, MD 20857
800-421-4211
www.nimh.nih.gov
E-mail: nimhinfo@nih.gov

NIMH is part of the National Institutes of Health and offers a considerable amount of information on depression. This "Public Information" page has links to Information on Specific Mental Disorders for very general information about specific disorders and to Depression Awareness Recognition Treatment Program for more detailed information and further useful topics (Women and Depression, Co-occurrence with Medical Conditions, and others).

National Library of Medicine
Clinical trials database
www.clinicaltrials.gov

National Mental Health Association
1021 Prince Street
Alexandria, VA 22314
800-969-NMHA (6642)
http://www.nmha.org

Provides the names and numbers of regional chapters and information on 200 mental health topics.

National Organization for Seasonal Affective Disorder (SAD)
P.O. Box 40133
Washington, DC 20016.

Names of light box companies and other information on seasonal affective disorder.

Society for Light Treatment and Biological Rhythms
842 Howard Avenue
New Haven, CT 06519
Fax: 203-764-4324
http://www.sltbr.org

ToDo Institute
P.O. Box 874
Middlebury, VT 05753
802-453-4440
http://www.todoinstitute.org
E-mail: todo@together.net

Provides a wide range of educational programs and services related to Constructive Living, Morita therapy, Naikan, Meaningful Life therapy, and other related areas.

Internet Newsgroups

Newsgroups are discussions that take place on the Internet. They can be accessed via the Internet by searching for "newsgroups" and then selecting the appropriate group. Depending on your "news reader" program (usually part of your Internet service provider's software package), the way that you communicate with these groups will vary.

soc.support.depression.crisis
soc.support.depression.family
soc.support.depression.manic
soc.support.depression.misc
soc.support.depression.seasonal
soc.support.depression.treatment
alt.support.depression.seasonal
alt.support.depression
alt.support.depression.manic
alt.support.depression.medication

More on the Internet

Cognitive Therapy
  http://www.cognitivetherapy.com

Depression FAQ
  http://depression.about.com/library/faqs/
  blfaqindex.htm?PM=ss13_depression

Frequently asked questions from the alt.support.depression newsgroup.

  http://depression/mentalhelp.net

Contains links to online support groups and some dysthymia specific information, in the symptom section.

Foods to avoid when taking MAOIs
  http://deoxy.org/maoidiet.html

Gratefulness.org

A nonprofit, education global network to inspire people to find in grateful living a transformative key to personal fulfillment.

http://gratefulness.org

http://www.mentalhealth.com/dis/p20-md04.html

Contains links to info on description, diagnosis, treatment, research, booklets, and magazine articles concerning dysthymia

Mental Health Online

http://www.mentalhealth.com

A free encyclopedia of mental health information.

http://www.cmhc.com/dxtx.htm
http://www.cmhc.com/bbs/forums.htm

Useful site with in-depth discussions of the various symptoms and treatments of different kinds of depression (major depressive disorder, major depressive episode, dysthymia, and bipolar disorder); many links to online resources and support services. Second Internet address goes to online forums where anyone can discuss mental health topics with others.

Mental Health Net
http://mentalhelp.net

Reuters Health
http://www.reutershealth.com

Information about virtually all FDA-approved drugs and some herbal supplements; use "drug database."

Therapists
http://www.1-800-therapist.com

Information on finding the right therapist.

References

"Acute Major Depression and Dysthymia: A Review of Newer Pharmacologic Agents." *Consultant* 40, 11: 1941, 2000.

Akiskal, H. S., and G. B. Cassano. *Dysthymia and the Spectrum of Chronic Depressions.* New York: Guilford Press, 1997.

American Psychiatric Association. *Diagnostic and Statistical Manual of Mental Disorders, 4th ed.* Washington, D.C.: American Psychiatric Association, 1994.

Artal, M., and C. Sherman. "Exercise Against Depression." *Physician and Sportsmedicine* 26, 10: 55–60, 1998.
http://www.physsportsmed.com/issues/1998/10Oct/artal.htm

Babyak, M., et al. "Exercise Treatment for Major Depression: Maintenance of Therapeutic Benefit at Ten Months." *Pychosomatic Medicine* 62, 5: 633–38, 2000.

Baker, B. "Simple Office Visits Help Mild Depression in Elderly." *Family Practice News* 30: 8, 2000.

Ballon, D. "Disorder of Discontent: Dysthymia Often Goes Ignored or Undertreated." *Journal of Addiction and Mental Health* 2, 4: 9, 1999.
http://www.camh.net/journal/journalv2no4/
disorder_discontent.html

Barkham, M., D. A. Shapiro, G. E. Hardy, and A. Rees. "Psychotherapy in Two-Plus-One Sessions: Outcomes of a Randomized Controlled Trial of Cognitive-Behavioral and Psychodynamic-Interpersonal Therapy for Subsyndromal Depression." *J Consult Clin Psychology* 67, 2: 201–11, 1999.

Barrett, J. E., J. W. Williams, T. E. Oxman, et al. "Treatment of Dysthymia and Minor Depression in Primary Care: A Randomized Trial in Patients Aged 18 to 59 years." *J Fam Pract* 50: 405–12, 2001.

Berndt, E. R., L. M. Koran, S. N. Finkelstein, A. J. Gelenberg, S. G. Kornstein, I. M. Miller, M. E. Thase, G. A. Trapp, and M. B. Keller. "Lost Human Capital from Early-Onset Chronic Depression." *Am J Psychiatry* 157, 6: 940–47, 2000.

Bloomfield, H. H., and P. McWilliams. *How to Heal Depression*. Los Angeles: Prelude Press, 1996.

Blumenthal, J. A., M. A. Babyak, K. A. Moore, et al. "Effects of Exercise Training on Older Patients with Major Depression." *Arch Intern Med* 159: 2349–56, 1999.

Brent, D. A., B. Birmaher, D. Kolko, M. Baugher, and J. Bridge. "Subsyndromal Depression in Adolescents after a Brief Psychotherapy Trial: Course and Outcome." *Journal of Affective Disorders* 63: 51–58, 2001.

Brody, J. "Quirks and Oddities May Be Mild Forms of Psychiatric Illness." *New York Times*, February 4, 1997.
http://www.english.upenn.edu/~afilreis/News/quirks.html

Burns, D. D. *Feeling Good: The New Mood Therapy*. New York: Signet, 1980.

———. *The Feeling Good Handbook: Using the New Mood Therapy in Everyday Life*. New York: William Morrow, 1989.

Bush, T. M., W. Katon, E.H.B. Lin, and E. J. Ludman, "Evidence-Based Treatment of Dysthymia in Primary Care: Case Study and Commentary." *J of Community Practice* 7, 6: 47, 2000.

Butcher, H. K. "A Unitary Field Pattern Portrait of Dispiritedness in Later Life." *J of Rogerian Nursing Science* 4: 41–58, 1996.

Byrne, A., and D. G. Byrne. "The Effect of Exercise on Depression, Anxiety, and Other Mood States: A Review." *J Psychosomat Res* 37: 565–74, 1993.

Callaway, E. "Dysthymic Disorder." *eMedicine Journal* 3, 1: January 17, 2002.
http://www.emedicine.com/med/topic3120

Center for Epidemiologic Studies, National Institute of Mental Health. *Center for Epidemiologic Studies Depression Scale (CES-D)*. Rockville, Md.: National Institute of Mental Health, 1971.

Coppen, A., and J. Bailey. "Enhancement of the Antidepressant Action of Fluoxetine by Folic Acid: A Randomised, Placebo Controlled Trial." *J Affective Disorders*. 60, 2: 121–30, 2000.

Curtis, A. B. *Depression Is a Choice: Winning the Right Without Drugs*. New York: Hyperion, 2001.

de Lima, M. S., M. Hotoph, and S. Wessely. "The Efficacy of Drug Treatments for Dysthymia: A Systematic Review and Meta-analysis." *Psychol Med* 29, 6: 1273–89, 1999.

de los Reyes, G., and R. T. Koda. "Determining Hyperforin and Hypericin Content in Eight Brands of St. John's Wort." *Am J Health-Syst Pharm* 59: 545–47, 2002.

DePaulo, J. R., and L. A. Horvitz. *Understanding Depression*. New York: John Wiley, 2002.

D'Epiro, N. W. "Chronic Depression: Now a Treatable Condition." *Patient Care* 34, 1: 56, 2000.

"Diagnosing and Treating Depression in the Elderly." *Women's Health in Primary Care* 1, 2: 196, 1998.

Doris, A., K. Ebmeier, and P. Shajahan. "Depressive Illness." *Lancet* 354 (9187): 1369–75, 1999.

Ellis, A. A. *The Essence of Rational Psychotherapy: A Comprehensive Approach to Treatment*. New York: Institute for Rational Living, 1970.

———. *How to Stubbornly Refuse to Make Yourself Miserable About Anything—Yes, Anything*. Secaucus, N.J.: Carol Publishing Group, 1988.

Ellis, A. A., and R. Harper. *A Guide to Rational Living*. North Hollywood, Calif.: Wilshire Book Company, 1976.

Empfield, M., and N. Bakalar. *Understanding Teenage Depression: A Guide to Diagnosis, Treatment, and Management*. New York: Holt, 2001.

Enright, R. D. *Forgiveness Is a Choice: A Step-by-Step Process for Resolving Anger and Restoring Hope*. Washington, D.C.: American Psychological Association, 2001.

Food and Drug Administration. "Dealing with the Depths of Depression." *FDA Consumer Magazine,* July-August 1998. http://www.fda.gov/fdac/features/1998/498_dep.html

Frank, E., and M. E. Thase. "Natural History and Preventative Treatment of Recurrent Mood Disorders." *Annu Rev Med* 50: 453–68, 1999.

Fugh-Berman, A., and J. M. Cott. "Dietary Supplements and Natural Products as Psychotherapeutic Agents." *Psychosom Med* 61, 5: 712–28, 1999.

Goldman, E. L. "Menopause Alone Won't Induce New-Onset Depression." *Family Practice News,* February 15, 2000. http://www.findarticles.com/cf_0/m0BJI/4_30/60579696/print.jhtml

Goleman, D. *Emotional Intelligence.* New York: Bantam, 1994.

Goodman, S. H. "Major Depression and Dysthymia in Children and Adolescents: Discriminant Validity and Differential Consequences in a Community Sample." *J American Academy of Child and Adolescent Psychiatry* 39: 761–70, 2000

Hartlage, S. A., K. E. Arduino, and S. Gehlert "Premenstrual Dysphoric Disorder and Risk for Major Depressive Disorder: A Preliminary Study." *J Clin Psychology* 57, 12: 1571–78, 2001.

Hatherleigh Guide to Managing Depression. New York: Hatherleigh Press, 1996.

Hayden, E. P., and D. N. Klein. "Outcome of Dysthymic Disorder at 5-year Follow-up: The Effect of Familial Psychopathology, Early Adversity, Personality, Comorbidity, and Chronic Stress." *American J Psychiatry* 158: 1864–70, 2001.

Hirschfeld, R. M., et al. "Does Psychosocial Functioning Improve Independent of Depressive Symptoms? A Comparison of Nefazodone, Psychotherapy, and Their Combination." *Biol Psychiatry* 51, 2: 123–33, 2002.

Hirschfeld, R. M., et al. "The National Depressive and Manic-Depressive Association Consensus Statement on the Undertreatment of Depression." *J American Medical Association* 277, 4: 333–40, 1997.

Hirschfeld, R. M., et al. "Predictors of Response to Acute Treatment of Chronic and Double Depression with Sertraline or Imipramine." *J Clin Psychiatry* 59, 12: 669–75, 1998.

Hollon, S. D., M. E. Thase, and J. D. Markowitz. "Treatment and Prevention of Depression." *Psychological Science in the Public Interest* 3, 2: 39–77, 2002.

Hypericum Depression Trial Study Group. "Effect of Hypericum Perforatum (St. John's Wort) in Major Depressive Disorder." *JAMA* 287, 14: 1807–14, 2002.

Jampolsky, G. G. *Love Is Letting Go of Fear.* Berkeley: Celestial Arts, 1979.

Judd, L. L. "Socioeconomic Burden of Subsyndromal Depressive Syndrome and Major Depression in a Sample of the General Population." *Am J Psychiatry* 153: 1411–417, 1996.

Kaplan, A. "Light Treatment for Nonseasonal Depression." *Psychiatric Times* 16, 3, 1999.

Keller, M. B., J. P. McCullough, D. N. Klein, et al. "A Comparison of Nefazodone, the Cognitive Behavioral-Analysis System of Psychotherapy, and Their Combination for the Treatment of Chronic Depression." *New Engl J Med* 342: 1462-70, 2000.

Keller, M. B., et al. "The Treatment of Chronic Depression, Part 2: A Double-Blind, Randomized Trial of Sertraline and Imipramine." *J Clin Psychiatry* 59, 11: 598–607, 1998.

Keller, M. B., et al. "Results of the DSM-IV Mood Disorders Field Trial." *Am J Psychiatry* 152, 6: 843–49, 1995.

Keller, M. B., et al. "Maintenance Phase Efficacy of Sertraline for Chronic Depression: A Randomized Controlled Trial." *JAMA* 280, 19: 1665–72, 1998.

Kessler, R. C., et al. "Lifetime and 12-month Prevalence of DSM-III-R Psychiatric Disorders in the United States. Results from the National Comorbidity Survey." *Arch Gen Psychiatry* 51: 8–19, 1994.

Kessler, R. C., et al. "The Use of Complementary and Alternative Therapies to Treat Anxiety and Depression in the United States." *Am J Psychiatry* 158, 2: 289–94, 2001.

King, A. C., et al. "Moderate-Intensity Exercise and Self-Rated Quality of Sleep in Older Adults. A Randomized Controlled Trial." *JAMA* 277, 1: 32–37, 1997.

Klaiber, E. L. *Hormones and the Mind: A Woman's Guide to Enhancing Mood, Memory, and Sexual Vitality.* New York: HarperCollins, 2001.

Klein, D. N., and E. P. Hayden. "Dysthymic Disorder: Current Status and Future Directions." *Current Opinion in Psychiatry* 13: 171–77. 2000.

Klein, D. N., J. E. Schwartz, S. Rose, and J. B. Leader. "Five-Year Course and Outcome of Dysthymic Disorder: A Prospective, Naturalistic Follow-up Study." *Am J Psychiatry* 157, 6: 931–39, 2000.

Klein, D. N., et al. "Age of Onset in Chronic Major Depression: Relation to Demographic and Clinical Variables, Family History, and Treatment Response." *J Affective Disorders* 55, 2–3: 149–57, 1999.

Kocsis, J. H., and D. N. Klein. *Diagnosis and Treatment of Chronic Depression.* New York: Guilford Press, 1995.

Koenig, H. G., L. K. George. and B. L. Peterson. "Religiosity and Remission of Depression in Medically Ill Older Patients." *Am J Psychiatry* 155, 4: 536–42, 1998.

Koran, L. M., et al. "Sertraline versus Imipramine to Prevent Relapse in Chronic Depression." *J Affective Disorders* 65, 1:27–36, 2001.

Kornstein, S. G., et al. "Gender Differences in Chronic Major and Double Depression." *J Affective Disorders* 60: 1–22. 2001.

Kornstein, S. G., et al. "Gender Differences in Treatment Response to Sertraline versus Imipramine in Chronic Depression." *Am J Psychiatry* 157, 9: 1445–52, 2000.

Kramer, P. D. *Listening to Prozac.* New York: Viking, 1993.

Kripke, D. F. "Brighten Your Life." http://www.brightenyourlife.info/ 2002

Kwon, J. S., et al. "Three-year Follow-up of Women with the Sole Diagnosis of Depressive Personality Disorder: Subsequent Development of Dysthymia and Major Depression." *Am J Psychiatry* 157: 1966–72, 2000.

Lamberg, L. "Dawn's Early Light to Twilight's Last Gleaming." *JAMA* 280: 1556–58, 1998.

Lecrubier, Y., P. Boyer, S. Turjanski, W. Rein. "Amisulpride Study Group. Amisulpride versus Imipramine and Placebo in Dysthymia and Major Depression." *J Affective Disorders* 43: 95–103, 1997.

Lecrubier, Y., G. Clerc, R. Didi, and M. Kieser. "Efficacy of St. John's Wort Extract WS 5570 in Major Depression: A Double-Blind, Placebo-Controlled Trial." *Am J Psychiatry* 159, 8: 1361–66, 2002.

Lima, M. S., and J. Moncrieff. "Drugs versus Placebo for Dysthymia (Cochrane Review)." *Cochrane Library* 1, 2002. Oxford: Update Software.

Linde, K., et al. "St. John's Wort for Depression—An Overview and Meta Analysis of Randomized Clinical Trials." *British Med J* 313, 7052: 253–58, 1996. Also comment in *British Med J* 313, 7066: 1204–5, 1996.

Lundervold, D. A. "Behavioral Counseling for Older Adults with Depression." In *Hatherleigh Guide to Managing Depression.* New York: Hatherleigh Press, 1996.

Markowitz, J. C. *Interpersonal Psychotherapy for Dysthymic Disorder.* Washington, D.C.: American Psychiatric Press, 1998.

———. "Recognizing and Treating Chronic 'Mild' Depression." *Women's Health in Primary Care* 2, 11: 855–61, 1999.

Mazure, C. M., G. P. Keita, and M. D. Blehar. *Summit on Women and Depression: Proceedings and Recommendations*. Washington, D.C.: American Psychological Association, 2002.
http://www.apa.org/pi/wpo/women&depression.pdf

McCullough, James P. *Treatment for Chronic Depression: Cognitive Behavioral Analysis System of Psychotherapy (CBASP)*. New York: Guilford Press, 2000.

McGuire, L., J. K. Kiecolt-Glaser, and R. Glaser. "Depressive Symptoms and Lymphocyte Proliferation in Older Adults." *J Abnormal Psychology* 111, 1: 192–97, 2002.
http://www.apa.org/journals/abn.html

Miller, I. W., et al. "The Treatment of Chronic Depression, Part 3: Psychosocial Functioning Before and After Treatment with Sertraline or Imipramine." *J Clin Psychiatry* 59, 11: 608-19, 1998.

National Institute of Mental Health. "Omega-3 Fatty Acids in Treatment of Major Depression and Bipolar Disorder: A Double-Blind Placebo-Controlled Study." *Clinical Research Study* (1999)-M-0181. Available at: http://www.clinicalstudies.info.nih.nimh. gov.cgi/detail.cgi?A_99-M-0181.html.

Nierenberg, A. A. "Full Remission: The New Standard for the Treatment of Depression." *J Clin Psychiatry* 60: 221–25, 1990.
http://www.depression.org.uk/main/infocentre/depression_center/treatgeneral7.pdf

Nierenberg, A. A., and E. C. Wright. "Evolution of Remission as the New Standard in the Treatment of Depression." *J Clin Psychiatry* 60 (suppl. 22): 7–11, 1990.

Norden, M. J. *Beyond Prozac: Brain-Toxic Lifestyles, Natural Antidotes and New Generation Antidepressants*. New York: Regan Books, 1996.

North, C., S. Nixon, S. Shariat, S. Mallonee, J. McMillen, E. Spitzanagel, and E. Smith. "Psychiatric Disorders among Survivors of the Oklahoma City Bombing." *JAMA* 282: 755–762, 1999.

O'Connor, R. *Undoing Depression: What Therapy Doesn't Teach You and Medication Can't Give You*. Boston: Little, Brown, 1997.

Olfson, M., et al. "National Trends in the Outpatient Treatment of Depression." *JAMA* 287: 203–9, 2002.

Philipp, M., R. Kohnen, and K. O. Hiller. "Hypericum Extract versus Imipramine or Placebo in Patients with Moderate Depression: Randomised Multicentre Study of Treatment for Eight Weeks." *British Med J* 319: 1534–53, 1999.

Ravindran, A. V., et al. Treatment of Primary Dysthymia with Group Cognitive Therapy and Pharmacotherapy: Clinical Symptoms and Functional Impairments. *Am J Psychiatry* 156: 1608–17, 1999.

Reynolds, D. *Constructive Living*. Honolulu: University of Hawaii Press, 1984.

Rihmer, Z. "Dysthymic Disorder: Implications for Diagnosis and Treatment. *Current Opinion in Psychiatry* 12, 1: 69–75, 1999.

Riso, L. P., R. K. Miyatake, and M. E. Thase. "The Search for Determinants of Chronic Depression: A Review of Six Factors." *J Affective Disorders* 70, 1: 103–15, 2002.

Rush, A. J., and M. E. Thase. "Strategies and Tactics in the Treatment of Chronic Depression." *J Clin Psychiatry* 58 (suppl. 13): 14–22, 1997.

Sansone, R. A., and L. A. Sasone. "Dysthymic Disorder: The Smoldering Depression." *Primary Care Reports* 7, 21: 1, 2001.

Seligman, M. *Authentic Happiness*. New York: Free Press, 2002.

———. *Learned Optimism: How to Change Your Mind and Life*. New York: Pocket Books, 1998.

———. *What You Can Change and What You Can't*. New York: Fawcett Columbine, 1993.

Shelton, R. C., M. B. Keller, A. Gelenberg, D. L. Dunner, R. Hirschfeld, M. E. Thase, J. Russell, R. B. Lydiard, P. Crits-Christoph, R. Gallop, L. Todd, D. Hellerstein, P. Goodnick, G. Keitner, S. M. Stahl, and U. Halbreich. "Effectiveness of St. John's Wort in Major Depression. A Randomized Controlled Trial." *JAMA* 285, 15: 1978–86, 2001.

Shelton, R. C., et al. "The Undertreatment of Dysthymia." *J Clin Psychiatry* 58, 2: 59–65, 1997.

Snow, V., S. Lascher, and C. Mottur-Pilson. "Pharmacologic Treatment of Acute Major Depression and Dysthymia." *Ann Intern Med* 132: 738–42, 2000.

Solomon, A. *The Noonday Demon: An Atlas of Depression*. New York: Scribner's, 2001.

Stahl, S. M. "Basic Psychopharmacology of Antidepressants, Part 2: Estrogen as an Adjunct to Antidepressant Treatment." *J Clin Psychiatry* 59 (suppl. 4): 15–24, 1998.

Stevens, T. G. *You Can Choose To Be Happy: "Rise Above" Anxiety, Anger, and Depression*. Seal Beach, Calif.: Wheeler-Sutton, 1998.

Stoll, A. L., W. E. Severus, M. P. Freeman, et al. "Omega-3 Fatty Acids in Bipolar Disorder. A Preliminary Double-Blind, Placebo-Controlled Ttrial." *Arch Gen Psychiatry* 56, 5: 407–12, 1999.

Swindoll, C. S. *Strengthening Your Grip*. Nashville, Tenn.: W Publishing Group (formerly Word, Inc.), 1982.

Thase, M. E. "Antidepressant Treatment of Dysthymia and Related Chronic Depressions." *Current Opinions in Psychiatry* 11: 77–83, 1998.

———. "Assessment of Depression in Patients with Chronic Fatigue Syndrome." *Rev Infect Dis* 13 (Suppl. 1): S114–18, 1991.

———. "Long-term Nature of Depression." *Clin Psychiatry* 60 (suppl. 14): 3–9, 31–35.

Thase, M. E., A. R. Entsuah, and R. L. Rudolph. "Remission Rates during Treatment with Venlafaxine or Selective Serotonin Reuptake Inhibitors." *British J Psychiatry* 178, 3:234–41, 2001.

Thase, M. E., E. S. Friedman, and R. H. Howland. "Management of Treatment-Resistant Depression: Psychotherapeutic Perspectives." *J Clin Psychiatry* 62 (suppl. 18): 18–24, 2001.

Thase, M. E., and R. H. Howland, "Assessment and Treatment of Chronic Depression." *Clin Adv in the Treatment of Psych* 9, 3: 1–11, 1995.

Thase, M. E., and E. E. Loredo. *St. John's Wort*. New York: Avon Books, 1998.

Thase, M. E., A. A. Nierenberg, M. B. Keller, and J. Panagides. "Efficacy of Mirtazapine for Prevention of Depressive Relapse: A Placebo-Controlled Double-Blind Trial of Recently Remitted High-Risk Patients." *J Clin Psychiatry* 62, 10: 782–88, 2001.

Thase, M. E., et al. "Double-Blind Switch Study of Imipramine or Sertraline Treatment of Antidepressant-Resistant Chronic Depression." *Arch Gen Psychiatry* 59, 3: 233–39, 2002.

Thase, M. E., et al. "A Placebo-Controlled, Randomized Clinical Trial Comparing Sertraline and Imipramine for the Treatment of Dysthymia." *Arch Gen Psychiatry* 53, 9: 777–84, 1996.

Tkachuk, G. A., and G. L. Martin. "Exercise Therapy for Patients with Psychiatric Disorders: Research and Clinical Implications." *Professional Psychology: Research and Practice* 30, 3. Full text of the article is available from the APA Public Affairs Office or at http://www.apa.org/journals/pro.html.

U.S. Department of Health and Human Services. *Mental Health: A Report of the Surgeon General—Executive Summary*. Rockville, Md.:

U.S. Department of Health and Human Services, Substance Abuse and Mental Health Services Administration, Center for Mental Health Services, National Institutes of Health, National Institute of Mental Health, 1999.
http://www.surgeongeneral.gov/library/mentalhealth/home.html

Versiani, M. "Pharmacotherapy of Dysthymic and Chronic Depressive Disorders: Overview with Focus on Moclobemide." *J Affective Disorders* 51: 769–74, 1998.

Wallis, M. A. "Looking at Depression Through Bifocal Lenses." *Nursing* 30: 58–61, 2000.

Wells, K. B., A. Stewart, R. D. Hays, et al. "The Functioning and Well-being of Depressed Patients. Results from the Medical Outcomes Study." *JAMA* 262: 914–19, 1989.

Williams, John W., et al. "Treatment of Dysthymia and Minor Depression in Primary Care: A Randomized Controlled Trial in Older Adults." *JAMA* 284: 1519–26, 2000.

Woelk, H. "Comparison of St. John's Wort and Imipramine for Treating Depression: Randomised Controlled Trial." *British Med J* 321: 536–39, 2000.

Yapko, M. D. *Breaking the Patterns of Depression*. New York: Doubleday, 1997.

Zweifel, J. E., and W. H. O'Brien. "A meta-analysis of the Effect of Hormone Replacement Therapy upon Depressed Mood [published erratum appears in *Psychoneuroendocrinology* 22, 8: 655, 1997]." *Psychoneuroendocrinology* 22, 3: 198–212.

Index